Scenes from Surgical Life

Scenes from
Surgical Life

DAVID LE VAY

Peter Owen · London

ISBN 0 7206 0384 6

PETER OWEN LIMITED
20 Holland Park Avenue London W11 3QU

First British Commonwealth edition 1976
© David Le Vay 1976

Printed in Great Britain by
Daedalus Press Stoke Ferry King's Lynn Norfolk

Acknowledgments

I should like to thank Mr Frederic Raphael and Sir Michael Tippett for kindly allowing me to include quotations from their work.

My thanks are also due to the following for permission to reproduce material: Cambridge University Press; Macmillan, London and Basingstoke; Faber and Faber Ltd; William Heinemann Ltd; Penguin Books Ltd; Schott and Co. Ltd; The Society of Authors.

Thackeray makes one of his footmen complain: 'Before you come to the book, there is, fust, a Deddication; then, a Preface; and nex', a Prolygominy. The fust is about hisself; the second about hisself, too; and, cuss me! if the Prolygolygominy ain't about hisself again.'

I can't help this book being about myself, since it is autobiographical. A dedication there has to be, but that is simple: 'To my Patients, because I need them far more than they need me.' We are now well into the preface; and I undertake that there shall be no Prolygolygominy.

The book originated in the autumn of 1973, during a period spent as Visiting Professor at the Medical School of Pahlavi University in Shiraz, Iran. I was alone and had a lot of time on my hands and kept a journal. I discovered that there were a number of things I had been wanting to put down which lack of leisure had previously denied an outlet; and on my return decided to expand the original diary by adding some reflections from a lifetime of surgical experience.

It will be apparent that my time in Shiraz coincided with one of those crises of middle life which most of us have to endure, and whose clinical course has been so incisively summed up by Samuel Beckett: I can't go on. I must go on. I go on.

If, in places, I have been tempted to ramble or digress, remember what Swift said: 'The Society of Writers would quickly be reduced to a very inconsiderable number if Men were put upon making Books with the fatal Confinement of delivering nothing beyond what is to the Purpose.'

I expose myself entire; 'tis a body where, at one view, the veins, muscles and tendons are apparent, every one of them in its proper place.

MONTAIGNE

Part One

Journey to Shiraz

29 October. Flying into evening, over the Alps towards Munich, the sunset a flaming ruin on our right. The new moon embraces an evening star, a premonition of the Crescent. Below, very close, are the Alps – stony, capped with snow and ice, with lakes and descending rivers. I am always terrified flying over mountains and think of Milton: 'O Lord, avenge thy slaughtered saints/Whose bones lie scattered on the mountains cold.' But in these clefts, so grey and hostile, are unexpected gleams of light, life clinging like a limpet even in these crevices. Foolish thoughts crowd my mind; if we crashed now, and survived, how is my German? *'Bitte, meine Flugmaschine ist kaput!'* The sunstreaks are almost gone now, the moon and its star bright against a magical blue, the aircraft's wing silhouetted like a great bat.

The jumbo-jet: democracy in air traffic to the nth degree. It is like a super-cinema, which, incidentally, it also is, by definition the most 'super' in the world. Babies and cots, children running, no decent, sober two-seated rows with a single aisle, no place for the slightly mysterious aloofness of the seasoned traveller. I could, if I wished, plug in to Bach or Mozart – how broadminded of British Airways to cater for minority tastes – but prefer not to. We are not on the ground, I am not listening to my own gramophone at home, I want to savour this experience to the full, and if I listen now either it or the music will suffer. This sounds remarkably sanctimonious. Is there, then, no earthly pursuit I should like to indulge in here, at 33,000 feet? Yes, to submit to the rules of free association, I should like to copulate with an unknown woman. There is something about air-travel – and space-travel – that favours the libidinal as a form of self-defence against the immensity and non-humanity of the universe. I well recall hearing or watching – it was many years ago – a programme on the vastnesses of space. It was awesome and reduced human life to less than a speck; and precisely because of this, immediately it was over, my wife and I made love without a word on the hearthrug.

13

Now it is night. The moon and star are brilliant to starboard. The wing has almost disappeared from view. A long haul still, three and a half hours, to Teheran. We seem to be taking the long way round, the length of Turkey, presumably to avoid overflying the Middle East, where the latest Israeli-Arab war has just ground to a standstill. Are we vulnerable to SAM missiles at 33,000 feet, assuming the Israelis have left any? This will have to be the last of these wars. As a Jew, I do not pretend to be impartial, but this waste and loss cannot continue. Neither side can afford it, particularly not the Israelis with their relatively tiny population. A real peace could transform the Middle East; Arab and Jew seem as complementary as husband and wife, made to work together to overcome poverty and disease and cultivate the wilderness. If this problem is insoluble, if the problem of Northern Ireland – another area where immigrants were deliberately brought in from outside to consolidate a contrived rearrangement of populations – is also insoluble, humanity might as well give up. And yet, despite the ravages of the Second World War and of subsequent wars, particularly in Vietnam, it seems that nationalism and local patriotism become more vigorous and virulent each day. It is like the copulation on the hearthrug: when everything is becoming more immense and impersonal, sanity depends on sticking to what we know. The citizen of the world is suddenly glad to take refuge by the parish pump.

And, of course, local patriotism is more natural and healthier, biologically regarded. Natural and evolutionary history shows that animals and man defend themselves primarily, their mates and families by extension, the community by further extension and identification. What's alien is hostile: ' 'Ere's a stranger, let's 'eave 'alf a brick at 'im !' That is how we survived. There is no place for altruism in evolution, at any rate there has not been till recently. Self-interest is the rule; the best we can hope for is that it should be enlightened. Even self-sacrifice is a form of self-interest, extended to the species. But we do seem to have got to a sticking point where we can only stand up for ourselves, express our paranoid determination not to be put upon, at the risk of blowing the planet to pieces. Biologically, emotionally, over-crowded harassed man yearns for another war; and dares not have one. The bomb, incidentally, has never worried me. It is equated with my own death: a thing I dare not contemplate with clear vision very often, or for very long.

Now the moon, too, is setting, the star stationary.

The children are milling round, the cinema screens have been run down. Where are we? Over Austria or possibly Bulgaria? Watching the film without sound – an advantage. It is a police-movie, made in Boston, which I recognize since I visited it – and America – for the first time eight months ago. It was like going to the moon. I had always vowed that I'd never want to set foot in the United States; but my son is a research neurobiologist in Harvard Medical School, so I combined a visit to him with a study tour of the orthopaedic clinics in the city. The movie is based on a novel I have read by Ed McBain, a writer to be respected because his work has authority, or at any rate, authenticity. A strange thing this, authority. It is the criterion of the true artist and even then, perhaps, not all of the time. Thus, in music, Bartok has absolute authority, always; Mozart very, very nearly always; certainly Stravinsky; Bach is beyond and above, Mahler has it where Bruckner has not. Can we apply this to painters and authors? I think so.

The moon, which is quite red now, is on the horizon. The film is over and the lights go up. Murder, rape and arson have prevailed on heaven as on earth. There was a new crime, too: the film showed muggers setting tramps on fire for kicks. And after it was shown in Boston, ruffians in that city began to do just that, to ordinary bourgeois civilians as well. What is the morality of making and showing a film like this? Its defenders will say that it only copies nature, its critics that nature copies art. If it is a circle, it is a vicious one. It hasn't made me want to go out and set fire to people, though I do admit to a certain catharsis; but I had read the book, and was forewarned. Perhaps these things would be better if they stayed in print; one doubts if the individuals who act out these fantasies can read, or read anything other than a comic book. But whose is the responsibility? We make such films, or allow them to be made and shown. We watch them and let our children watch them, under what the censor's certificate euphemistically calls 'Parental Guidance' – 'No, dear, being burnt alive doesn't really hurt and the lady doesn't really mind what the man is doing to her, she is only pretending to scream.' We watch our troops – yours and mine – setting women and children on fire with napalm. Burn, baby, burn! Is it any wonder that the line blurs between fiction and reality, between what is permissible and what is criminal?

An hour and a half to Teheran. Over Turkey. I could get the taste of the film out of my mouth by plugging in to the classical music hour. But that is a contrast that is not permissible, to be a beast at one moment and an angel the next. It would be like the behaviour of a friend who watches all-in wrestling with the sound turned off and Bach's unaccompanied cello suites on the hi-fi. . . . It recalls an occasion when I was complaining to a colleague in the French provinces about the horrors of television; of how, on Bloody Saturday, when my wife and I and young family were having tea, the screen showed us bleeding chunks of human meat being shovelled into sacks on the streets of Belfast. 'Yes,' he said seriously, I do not know how seriously, 'that's why I've moved the television from the dining-room into the sitting-room!'

Teheran. Met by the charming young wife of my Persian assistant in London. In the dark, a vast featureless plain of a city, empty now at midnight, warm as an English June though it is nearly November. I am deposited at a hotel, dingy on the outside but revealing itself within as worthy of its name, Semiramis. Very opulent, with corresponding prices for a palatial suite with the largest and most ornate television set I have ever seen. The radio is playing delicious oriental music – the sort of music I should like to have in the theatre when I am operating, most operations being so boring. I'm sure that music makes surgery, like driving, more relaxed. I fall asleep reading tales of the Sufis.

Morning brings mild depression, despite the heat and glitter and bustle, the light glaring after the mild English autumn. Faces, crowds, hooded women, announce this is the East. The faces are interesting. All the time one seems to see replicas of the Shah, that keen, hawklike visage, as if the Monarch were literally the Father of his people. And he himself is everywhere, with wife and child, on posters and photographs in the shops. Other types of face emerge – Semitic, Turkish, Tartar. I suppose foreigners must find it difficult to pick out individual differences among what Orwell calls 'the mild knobby faces' of the English. My hostess arrives after breakfast and bears me off in a taxi. The cabs are really substitutes for a metro or an efficient municipal bus service here. Anyone can flag one down, no matter who is already in occupation, and will be accepted if his route is coincident with or not wildly divergent from that of the majority, just as is the case in Turkey and Israel. So we proceed in a series of swoops and starts, bearing down with an inquiring toot of the horn, but never quite stopping, on an individual or a knot of people who hopefully shout their destination and are waved in, or away, as the case may be. It's like swallows diving to sup an insect, or the kites that once descended when I was eating a sandwich in the garden of a Delhi hotel, snatched my morsel in passage, and were away. The driving is French – no, Belgian – in its dash and brutality, swerving from lane to lane, all brake and clutch. After a time one ceases to cling to the door-handle and accepts it fatalistically. But I'm informed that there are a lot of accidents here; and blood-transfusions cost ten pounds a litre! That really sounds like a tale for travellers; I must check when I get to Shiraz.

We go to the Flower Garden Square where there are a magnificent museum and palace, notable for halls of mirrors, Persian tiles and carved marble, some 19th century paintings of interiors which, though showing French influence, give a real impression of Persian domestic life, and a fascinating folk-lore section that gives an illuminating but probably increasingly backward look at daily life and customs.

All this is being written while taking off to Shiraz, which, having been a far-off Mecca during a year of negotiations, letters, telegrams and even telephone-calls, now seems to have a good chance of merging into reality. The little sheds along the runway are shaped exactly like the kiosks in the paintings this morning. Up now, haze, a tawny landscape. My palms sweat; shall I ever get used to flying? I swear to come back at the end of my tour by ship or train.

Now we descend over the red lunar landscape, bank sharply round the end of a mountain range, and behold an oasis – green gardens with tall cypresses springing from the plain, signs of irrigation spread over a wide area, more and more buildings, minarets – Shiraz. It is wonderful to see after hundreds of miles of desert, and must have been more wonderful still to those who once approached it on foot or camel-back. This time no one is waiting for me. The taxi goes straight as an arrow for several miles down an approach avenue lined by tall trees, with roses in full bloom all down its central axis. At the old comfortable Park Hotel, whose owner is the father-in-law of the sister of my assistant's wife, and where I had been promised a welcome, my first check. There is no room; and this is where I had confidently expected one and had intended to stay until my situation clarified. Apparently negotiations had been opened but not, from their point of view, concluded. So tonight I must stay elsewhere, at the International, which is newer and grander, and settle in at the Park tomorrow. Another hair-raising drive. It is a sort of *machismo*; you stay on a collision course until the last possible moment, and the one who gives way loses face.

Cypresses, a warm, dry golden sunlight, a high sky, a faint breeze. These – I can dispense with the cypresses – are my essential ingredients for happiness on this earth; though oddly, in England, I also enjoy a lowering cloudy sky and a warm south-west wind with a hint of rain. One need not have come so far for these delights. They are available in the corner of rural France where I intend to retire. It is the English damp that rots the bones and makes the spirit sodden, that and the density of the population. One cannot be properly human – or, for that matter, properly animal, as many experiments have shown – under overcrowded conditions. The meekest creatures will turn and rend each other if herded in too close proximity; we all need a physical, a spiritual territory of our own. Sunset, five o'clock, the hour of the bath and the aperitif. I will consider myself on holiday until tomorrow; but it is a dull evening, in an empty TV-dominated lounge, enlivened only by vodka and lime, the local speciality.

Next day. A baptism of fire, beginning, leisurely enough, with a stroll across town to the Park Hotel. Any description I give of the city must sound naïve nowadays, when package tours have opened the world to everyone. Still, it seems that to be in Shiraz for the autumn just now is for the relatively elect: only a few English and German tourists to be seen. The air bracing and exhilarating at six thousand feet. Dust. The wonderful quality of the light. Flocks of sheep and goats. Veiled women and girls with miniskirts side by side, the occasional squatter on the spittle-streaked pavements. A certain amount of glitter, of tawdriness; but, on the whole, the Zand, the great boulevard which transects Shiraz from east to west, has far less than one would expect of the heterogeneous *dreck* that litters the avenues of most western cities. An English bookshop by the hotel, thank God, the BBC office next-door closed down by the wrath of the Shah for insolence in a radio interview. I settle in like a dog, turn

round and round in my room, unpack. All, as will be shown, possibly
a waste of effort.

Report to the Pahlavi University Medical School, back along the
Zand, where everything happens. A courteous reception from the
Dean and an immediate introduction to Dr Z., a ball of fire, director
of the hospital as well as orthopaedic surgeon. It is one of life's bless-
ings that an orthopaedic surgeon who encounters his like anywhere
in the world has met a blood-brother. We have the same problems,
the same frustrations, the same recalcitrant flesh to wrestle with; we
love and hate our work, the patients drain us dry. We *know* what
each other's life is like. Dr Z. takes me to lunch, pours out his joys,
his sorrows, tells me of his love for England, where he spent his training years, of how the work has caught up on him in middle age –
he is only fifty to my fifty-eight, but they age faster here – and how
the only thing he really enjoys is hunting boar. I nod sympatheti-
cally, knowing it all from within, having heard it all from orthopaedic surgeons in Bombay and Boston, Copenhagen and Khartoum.

Back at the Hospital, I am informed that a flat is available at a
much cheaper rate than the hotel; so I must move again tomorrow. I
am taken to a fifth-year student seminar by Dr Z. and make my bow.
I apologize for my lack of Farsi, ask them to make use of my experience, and join in the discussion. They are an impressive group, well-
dressed, well-behaved, their English tolerable – all the teaching at
this university is in English – but very bookish. I find I have forgotten undergraduates and their needs, having been so long away
from a teaching hospital; must avoid the tendency to talk down, to
play the great surgeon. It's evident that I shall probably learn more
from them, or from teaching them, than they from me.

A tour of the Hospital, which is in process of being torn down and
reconstructed while work continues. I suddenly realize, confronted
with the patients, how *Moslem* this world is, which makes me
slightly uncomfortable. After all, Damascus is probably not so very
different; and I would not go down well there at all at this moment
in history. More introductions. An assistant is assigned to me. Tomorrow starts with a bang at another hospital at 7.30, then conferences and more conferences. On Monday I have to give my first
formal lecture.

Evening of the first day. The son of the hotel proprietor and his

wife, an elegant young woman trained in child guidance and soci-
ology in America, entertain me to dinner. I have to apologize for
having to leave tomorrow after promising a long stay; they know it
all already. Then a tour of Shiraz by night: stars, gardens, mountains, palaces, bazaars, the Koran Gate. I desperately want to be back
at the hotel, where they are trying to make a telephone connection
with my wife, who must be getting worried at having received no
word after forty-eight hours. But it is clear that international calls
from here are like arrows winged into the dark. Shoulders are
shrugged. Maybe. It all depends on the determination of the
operator, how everyone is feeling. I urge their efforts, unhopefully;
if the call does not materialize tonight I will send a wire in the morning.

1 November. Whisked away at 7.30 to the Nemazee Hospital for a
lecture and ward-rounds. This is a very modern centre, built on
American money, and the talk, by a visiting American fireman, is
very high-powered indeed. Gradually realize that, instead of being
the passive receptive person I normally am, I have to fill the role of
the foreign sage, to opine, to pontificate, to lend authority to one or
other side in a clinical argument; hope this went off satisfactorily.
Back to Saadi Hospital: an interminable business meeting of the surgical faculty discussing the merits of this or that resident or student.
All in English, for my benefit, with a tendency to lapse into the vernacular when heated. How must these Iranians feel at having to conduct their internal affairs in a foreign language, as a matter of policy?
As I say, it breaks down when emotions are stirred, but what a tribute,
however unwillingly paid. But there is not the slightest sign of this.
After all, it is not like having to speak German under a German occupation, or English in British India; it is a matter of election.

I break down, too, when taken along to the flat prepared for me
opposite the hospital. I suddenly realize that I simply can't set up
housekeeping for myself, alone in a country where I don't speak a
word of the language, where I can't even use the telephone. I yearn
for the fleshpots, and the infra-structure, of the Park Hotel – where,
incidentally, the owner has paid for my night's stay – for its support
system of managers and waiters, bar and restaurant. I feel it's my only
link with back home, that perhaps that telephone call will come
through after all. Finally baulk and tell the hospital manager – we

have discovered that we both speak passable French – that it won't do. It's not really his affair, he is only carrying out faculty instructions, so he lends me an ambulance with a driver in which we return to the hotel. My room is still vacant, my bags still there; I stay. What relief! The bar, talking to other English people, a nap after lunch: I am a tourist again. Something is wrong somewhere, however, and I know what it is. I can't, at my age, live entirely on my own.

Dusk, very rapid, soon after five. The mountains that ring the town are sharply etched, turn from tawny to purple. This is the hour for strolling on the Zand. Gossiping soldiers walk with little fingers intertwined, the bakers fire their ovens, a muezzin calls, it is the eve of Friday, everyone is relaxed and happy. Except me. My self-sufficiency has taken a knock. I am more dependent on other people than I had realized. Probably this anxious period will pass, it is the realization of commitment, that I have to go through with it. But how I overrated my resources; a month here with my wife would have been one thing, a shared adventure, three months on my own is quite another. The working days will take care of themselves, it is the evenings and short weekends that are the problem. But I'm no worse off than a typist or secretary at home, who doesn't talk to a soul from five o'clock in the evening till nine the next morning. The fact is that I'm an unusually dependent and immature person who resents his dependency, has never quite grown up. Who has? Trite thoughts about wives and companionship make it clear it's time for a vodka, the cheapest drink in these parts.

Saved, at the bell, by another Dr Z., who carries me off to a magnificent dinner at his home. He and his young wife look back with nostalgia to their days in Exeter, in Cheltenham, in Nottingham. How can they? 'Of course, it's true you have winter ten months in the year, but England is so nice.' And this in a country where one can sit out of doors on a November evening, and the stars are brilliant in an unclouded sky. Dr Z. shows me a carpet he has just bought for £2,000. Three or four other carpets are piled up in a corner. There is a maid – an old woman – to do the washing-up. He scoffs at my salary and I think of how we live at home, the overdraft, the total absence of domestic help. There was a dashing young neurosurgeon at dinner, home from Johns Hopkins in Baltimore. We discuss cases till it is time to leave.

Friday 2 November. Everything seems *en fête.* Stroll round the bazaar – like any other Eastern bazaar – and some mosques. Alas, my resolutions founder – not to drink, not to smoke, not to eat more than one meal a day. After lunch, sun-bathing on the balcony, almost too fierce to stand at three in the afternoon. So I sit in the garden under the trees, translating Monique Wittig's *Le Corps Lesbien,* very anatomical and remarkable. About sunset a great inrush and twittering of sparrows, flying and diving, but only in the planes, not the cypresses. I've often noticed this twilight chorus in towns, the play before bedtime, not much commented on by ornithologists, then a sudden hush as night falls. Then the bar, one vodka-tonic, then another, conversation with an engineer, cigarettes. End the evening thoroughly narcotized, and perhaps not such a bad thing.

3 November. A typical Monday-morning feeling, though it's Saturday. Looking at last night's notes, I see I must have been drunk – Ali is very generous with his vodka. Today a pattern begins to emerge. After breakfast – indoors or under the trees – one walks along the Zand. The Medical School and Saadi Hospital are a pleasant twenty-minute sunshiny stroll away, the Nemazee a further fifteen minutes to where the Zand comes to a dead end, so I shall get plenty of exercise. The mountains hem in the town closely on all sides; the buildings run right up to the foothills. It reminds me of the year I spent in Geneva working with the World Health Organization at a time when strains of divorce and remarriage made a change of scene imperative. But there the mountains are rather farther out and an official Swiss grey-blue, instead of this lion colour, and often invisible. It was strange, that year, a temporary secondment as far as my Hospital Board was concerned, a probationary first year as WHO saw it: an ideally open-ended arrangement for me. The transition from surgeon to editor was smooth enough, for I had written extensively throughout my surgical career. Indeed, right at the outset I had to choose between a tempting editorial post and my hospital consultancy; I would have settled for the former if they had let me retain even one clinical half-day a week, but not so. In the event I never regretted opting for surgery, not when I was poised to plunge into hectic overwork in a London suburb which had never had an orthopaedic surgeon before. It held all the excitement of a new love-affair, a new country; never was life so pleasant – this was before the National Health Service – and never did I feel that

I was being paid so much for doing something I so much enjoyed.

At the Saadi, in the morning, an exhaustive and exhausting briefing on my future timetable. I notice my anxiety as successions of new facts are announced. Can I absorb them, can I discharge these duties? By dint of chain-smoking I do absorb them, am surprised in fact by my ability in middle-age to acquire and store new knowledge; but I write everything down carefully.

Tour the buildings. A confirmation of my theory that one should never try consciously to learn a lay-out or a geography or a language, merely expose oneself to it. Things adhere, sink in. I learn the whereabouts of the various departments by strolling through them, like a child in the house it grows up in. I'm even, after four days, beginning to be able to read the numbering on the doors and coins, a very ancient system which antedates ours and gave it birth.

After lunch a siesta, then to the Nemazee where one of the orthopaedic surgeons wants my advice. A man of forty, a well-to-do private patient and friend of the surgeon, has been treated for five weeks for a fracture below the knee. After all this time he is discovered also to have a fracture of the thigh-bone, very badly angulated. My friend is much chagrined; I sympathize, we have all had such experiences. But he has to explain it somehow to the patient and break the news that a major operation is necessary – after five weeks during which the man had thought he was getting better. We discuss the most suitable technique. I am in favour of passing a long nail through the marrow cavity of the two fragments from end to end of the bone and he reluctantly agrees. Having given this advice, I am committed to lending a hand with the operation at seven tomorrow morning. Seven! When at home I've never been able to persuade my staff to start a minute earlier than 8.30, however long the list, however hot the day. If you start operating at seven you can get an enormous amount of work done by lunchtime; if you start late, Parkinson's Law begins to operate and fills the whole languid day till evening. When I visit my colleagues in the USA, in Denmark, France or Switzerland, I have to be there at seven, whatever the time of year. It frees the afternoon for other demands, for private patients or for relaxation. All sorts of excuses are made by my staff – the porters won't come so early, the instruments can't be got ready so soon, the cleaners won't have finished. They do not obscure the real reason, which is that the English are damned lazy.

Evening. Collapse again, vodka, an unwanted dinner. I remind myself that I am not on holiday. It's only in the last year or two that I've begun to feel the need for a large drink at the end of the day, and for cigars. Still, I prepare a lecture and find, in the next-door bookshop, still open at 9 p.m., a copy of Flaubert's *Salammbô,* which I have always wanted to read. I happen also to have brought with me Livy's account of the wars against Hannibal; they should make a good pair.

Sunday 4 November. Breakfast at 6.30, a chilly half-hour's walk, the sun not yet risen. Of course, having got to the operating theatre early, I now see the other side of the picture. Just as in the States, *because* everyone is early, there is incredible dawdling and delay in the anaes-thesia, the preparation of the patient, leisurely rituals of skin-painting and towelling. The first operation actually begins at 8.45. This is the American style, and so is the surgery itself – gradual, deliberate, fussy, pauses for discussion. We may start later in Britain, but once we are under way we get on with it. The preparation of this leg took a good half-hour; it would have taken me two minutes. Americans are always amazed, and often incredulous, when told that procedures that take them two or three hours are regularly completed in an hour in my theatre in London. We make far less fuss and are faster and surer in our methods, though there are exceptions. Perhaps this is a hangover from our long pre-anaesthetic surgical history when speed was essen-tial and an amputation of the thigh – 'Time me, gentlemen!' – could be done in twenty seconds or so. Anaesthesia abolished the need for haste, and most of America's surgical history dates from after the dis-covery of ether anaesthesia. In my experience Americans are slow in all things. They certainly work hard, as far as elapsed hours are con-cerned, and with an almost Teutonic application and thoroughness, but they lack pace. They are always amazed to see me dispose of an outpatient clinic of fifty or sixty patients in a couple of hours, which is possible if one concentrates on essentials and keeps the courtesies to a minimum. But the Americans are great on superficial courtesy, and the Persians seem to follow their example rather than ours.

Once the skin has been incised I am at home. The place, the lan-guage and colour of the skin are strange; but within is the familiar anatomy, the same old friends – muscles, nerves, blood-vessels – in the same places all over the world. Hence the brotherhood of surgery; the problems are identical because they arise in identical structures, and the techniques used to deal with them must also be the same. As my

Persian friend handles his instruments he is as conditioned as I am by the material with which he has to work, faces the same difficulties, feels the same anxieties. He is tense, calls for a sweatband. Watching, I am as cool as a cucumber, advise gravely and pontifically; but if it were I who were doing the operation, it is I who would be sweating. Afterwards he thanks me profusely for my support; but I gave him nothing that he did not already possess.

The question of surgical tension is a fascinating one. No one but a surgeon knows what it is like, not even doctors who are not surgeons. I have heard physicians opine that surgery must be very like carpentry; but the truest word came from a surgeon who began life as an anaesthetist. 'When I was an anaesthetist,' he used to say, 'I wondered what all the fuss and bother at the other end was about. Now I know.' The basic fact is that surgery is an unnatural and essentially *forbidden* procedure, a mutilating attack on the human body, albeit for therapeutic reasons. What the surgeon actually does to another person with his knife is, in itself, punishable in all societies by law, sometimes by death. The fact that it is carried out with good intentions and with society's approval does not and cannot remove the unconscious importance attached to this breaking and entering into the human body; and I have always profoundly believed that surgical practice generates more or less intense guilt, more or less unconscious, quite apart from, and added to, the normal decent responsibility the surgeon feels towards his patient. If you cut a man, he may die; it is as simple as that. The psychoanalytical associations and fantasies in the surgeon's mind are enormous, as I know very well from my own lengthy psychoanalysis.

'The unique alchemy of surgery in general, and perhaps of orthopaedic surgery in particular, lies in its power to afford an orthodox, nay a socially laudable transmutation into beneficent activity of destructive and aggressive impulses from the depths of personality. A permitted violation of the taboo on mutilation of the human body leads to a triumphant transfiguration of the darker side of human nature.'* I do not want to elaborate this further; many of my colleagues will differ profoundly, see this view as absurd, others may know intuitively that I am right. It is not arguable.

It seems somehow pertinent to quote Baudelaire's remark here: 'Love closely resembles a torture or a surgical operation . . . one of the

* David Le Vay, *The Life of Hugh Owen Thomas.* E. & S. Livingstone, 1956.

two is always more placid, or less obsessed, than the other. He or she is the operator or the executioner; the other is the subject, the victim.'

Am taken to see a patient who has been admitted under my care, a 'super-private patient'. Good, for I'm on short commons out here, the salary being less than half what I earn at home so that, in effect, I am paying heavily to be here at all and certainly can't afford a stay of more than three months. But a glance at the patient expels any mercenary considerations. An angelic-looking girl of nine with masses of curly hair, she has had a pain in the loin for nearly a year, which has been much investigated, and diagnosed as a 'behaviour disorder'. The parents had been on the point of flying her out to see me in London until my visit made this unnecessary. The examination and the X-rays, though not absolutely definite, are pretty conclusive. She has a spinal tumour which has replaced the body of the second lumbar vertebra, is producing paralysis of the legs and a swelling of the back. So much for the 'behaviour problem'. But then it always pays to be last on the scene in a case difficult to diagnose, for by then the signs have become so much more obvious. Soon after I was first appointed as a consultant I made my reputation by saving the life of the young son of a well-esteemed local general practitioner. He had been desperately ill with a high fever for two weeks and had been seen by some very eminent people, but no diagnosis had been made. By the time I saw him the condition had localized down to a very clear infection of the hip-bone, and operation gave an excellent result. But if I had seen him at the beginning of those two weeks, I should have been as puzzled as my senior colleagues; the laity do not realize sufficiently that often, in matters of diagnosis, one must literally 'wait and see'.

During the examination the little girl clings desperately to her underpants, then, when persuaded to relinquish these, covers her private parts protectively with both hands. I have seen this all over the world. Castration complex? I say 'Salaam aleikoum' gravely to the mother, thinking that it is identical with the Hebrew 'Shalom aleichem' and how much better it would be for the Middle East if Jews and Arabs could exchange this greeting instead of bullets. We shall have a few more X-ray investigations and then I shall explore her back. If we are wrong, if this is an infection and we find pus, what joy! But I fear that this is unlikely, that there will be a solid malignancy; and, if so, she is going to die quickly, but not quickly enough, painfully, probably with incontinence of bowels and bladder, with merciful final coma. And there is nothing we can do about it.

Evening, a university party. A crowd of guests from different faculties, mostly medical, the English wives (former nurses) of Iranian physicians and surgeons, much chit-chat about old times. Manners and English flawless. Several Americans, with the keenness, drive, wit, intellect and self-assuredness that make me feel like a visitor from a minor planet. Food and drink superb in quantity and quality. I love this kind of party and reverence (why?) academics, probably part of a pattern of feeling an intellectual *manqué*. How nice to end my days as one of them, after three decades of slogging suburban surgery in London. I realize I am beginning to be happy here and that I haven't had anything like this positive feeling for many years. Am treated with respect, even deference, the VIP out of the clouds with much knowledge to impart, if not power, treated with courtesy and charm. It seems meant, not superficial; so my ego blossoms, this seems my rightful place. And people generally behave as they are treated and expected to behave. Ignored, unappreciated, they contract, become mean-spirited, unambitious; treated with respect and appreciation, they expand like a magnolia flower in the morning sun. And so with me. I *am* a better person here, feel more human, more self-confident, think and act more usefully and economically because a road that seemed barred has opened; I can move forward and develop after what seems to have been a quarter of a century of stagnation.

Monday 5 November. A chillier morning, the day shorter, but the sun fierce at noon. What I wrote last night now seems naïvely lyrical. Walking to the hospital one sees blocks of ice delivered at the doorstep like milk, melting and trickling slowly over the pavements as the sun catches them. Struck again by the slow pace of my colleagues' operating: I'll swear I can do the same work in a quarter of the time. But then we do long lists, concentrate our work into, say, two days a week; here they spread it over the whole week, with only one or two cases a morning. The medical library has a superb collection of journals, and the students using it are much like medical students anywhere. I have to give a grand lecture on total replacement of the hip-joint in two weeks' time and collect material; that won't be too bad, as it will be to equals, but I am thoroughly nervous about my reception by the seventy or so third-year students to whom I have to talk tomorrow morning. Dr Z. hints they may rag me a bit and will stand by to see fair play.

My first outpatient clinic this afternoon. As in the operating theatre, considerations of colour, caste and language become of no account, though I do have a senior student as interpreter. Injuries of knee cartilages, club-feet, the same as at home. But there are also far more cases of severe bone infection than we ever see, and terrible scarring and deformities from burns in children. All the patients are grateful for my attentions and say so, clasping my hand. That's also a rarity in England now. When I was first consultant in a London hospital before the National Health Service, gratitude *was* a commonplace and Christmas saw the consulting-room piled with gifts; now that I am paid by the State I am used – and abused – as a State servant accordingly and from one years' end to another rarely receive more than a couple of letters of thanks. Not that I want them; I am uncomfortable when thanked and rebuff it brusquely. Here all the patients seem to have to pay something for their visit, their X-rays, their pathology tests, so they value them as we, often, do not. Further, because many of them are poor, one does not indulge here in the battery of extensive and expensive tests we apply so freely in England, a shotgun method of bringing down a diagnosis without taking proper aim or using true clinical acumen. Here one has to restrict oneself to the few essential tests that may really help, for the patient will need all the money he has got to keep himself alive while unable to work, to pay for his drugs, his plaster cast or his operation.

A 'death conference' at five. Very very good indeed. A splendid pathology department, very high standards, not easily bettered anywhere. Then, as it's Guy Fawkes night, fireworks, sausages and beer at the British Council. I am invited to visit the Mission Hospital, run by an English doctor and his wife, on Friday. But I must do something about getting to Persepolis too; I daren't leave here without having seen it, like a Londoner who has never visited the Tower.

Rather dejected tonight. Grasp at the opportunity of making any English acquaintance, but it's not enough.

Thursday 6 November. My first lecture, to seventy students in their first clinical year, is over. If not a howling success, it was not for lack of howling on their part at my late arrival, though Dr Z. was there to quieten them down and after that all went smoothly. We were late because Dr Z. did not arrive to fetch me as arranged; the reason emerged as soon as I had flagged down a taxi already holding five passengers. One half of the Zand was closed for repairs, the other half choked with morning rush-hour traffic, cars even driving in opposite directions in the same lane. The relief after the talk was so great that I realize how much I have been dreading it, as so often at home after a long clinic or difficult operation. Students crowd round for private conversation, all helpful, all courteous; I've yet to come across bad manners or discourtesy. Still, it's only a week.

Between lectures, in the glorious sunshine, refreshment at an outdoor kiosk in the grounds of the Medical School. Discover, with great delight, that here one can buy one cigarette at a time instead of having to get – and use – an unwanted whole packet. I recall that, when young, it was possible to buy for a penny one Churchman's in a little packet from railway station slot-machines.

More students in the wards; and I realize, rather late, that I am teaching them at postgraduate level. One can never be too simple. My curly-haired child has recovered from an arduous and painful X-ray session yesterday. I talk a little with her father, a businessman, and somehow the fact emerges that I have nine sons. 'May Heaven bless them all! May your shadow never grow less!' he intones solemnly. I do not mention my two daughters and will be reprimanded for this when I get home. But I do not tell him that *his* daughter is going to die, and would not have done even had it been possible to hold a fluent conversation. Yet at some stage I shall have to implant the seeds of despair in these trusting parents – after the operation, when we have the pathological report on the removed tissue.

Afternoon – more seminars, conferences, more opportunity to pontificate, I *do* seem to know a lot about my subject, am thanked and congratulated. This raises an important point, that human beings are so constructed that it is impossible for them to give themselves, physically or spiritually, a pat on the back. If we were really mature we might not need this, but who is? We all need our egos massaged, however rarely, or our spinal cords will shrivel up – need to feel that we are not alone in the universe, that there is someone, someone superior, who notices and approves of us.

7 November. Woke feeling as ill as I felt well yesterday. Gloom and despair. It seemed an unwelcome return of depression, but during the morning the reason becomes clear, an acute attack of traveller's diarrhoea. This causes considerable malaise and disturbance, to be solved only by determining the whereabouts of the strategic lavatories – not easy as no diagrams on doors – and carrying wads of toilet-paper in an inside pocket. This condition is universal and remains something of a medical mystery. To some extent it affects more often travellers from west to east, or north to south, from more hygienic to less hygienic places. But this is by no means the whole story; it is a matter of not being used to the local viruses. There is no real method of prophylaxis and no modern drugs are much better in treatment than old-fashioned chalk and opium. As I already – like Freud – suffer from an irritable colon, it is a plague from which I am never really free throughout my stay in Iran; and many prove to be the social functions I have to quit hurriedly, and in anguish, to squat in solitude on the porcelain footprints of a Persian lavatory. Travellers are often warned against other disorders acquired from food and water – hydatid disease, amoebiasis and the rest – and reminded of the risks of un-washed salads. But I cannot live with these precautions and decide to become naturalized and run the local risks; this is in contrast with my short stay in India, where I never got used to the crowds, dirt and fear of infection. Have to lie down at the hotel at midday. It is interesting that, in people prone to depression, and often even in others, acute illness or a surgical operation frequently unleashes the black dog, sometimes suicidally.

Drag myself to a seminar at 3.30 and glad of it. Very impressed once more by the calibre of these students, at least as good as our own. Find myself fluent and didactic; and as amazed as ever at the sparks of wit and wisdom that can be struck by contact with others when internally one feels dark and empty. Some human contact seems necessary to elicit purposefulness and socially useful thoughts and actions which would otherwise be not only unexpressed but, strangely, unfelt and unrecognized. I experience, too, the rare but grateful feeling of teaching, a warm useful outgoing sensation felt physically in the chest. I dislike psychoanalysis and psychoanalytic interpretations; neverthe-less, I can only say that it seems to me to compare with the feelings of a woman suckling her child. And teaching is the *only* activity that makes me feel like this.

8 November. Seen on the Zand at midday: men on their haunches puffing at a hookah; roadworkers squatting in a circle, each with his little black tea-kettle on the charcoal fire; the local equivalent of fish and chips – enormous steaming cauldrons of some root vegetable (white beet?) eaten on the spot with plate and fork; a shop-sign – MENS GLUB EMOTION HERMES – which I could decipher with a little application but prefer to contemplate as it stands. A woman in black, squatting on the pavement outside the hospital, is bellowing rhythmically like an animal in pain, clawing furrows in her face with the nails of both hands, tearing out her hair. What she is doing seems mechanical and repetitive, but there is no doubt about the depth of her despair. Someone – a husband or child – is dying or dead in the hospital. She is surrounded by a ring of onlookers, mute and sympathetic; they do not try to restrain her. And why should they? She is expressing her grief *now,* with every fibre and gland and muscle in her body. It is a splendid exercise in mental hygiene, compared with the civilized restraint in face of grief that burdens our bosoms with the perilous stuff. Truly and fully to express through one's body what one feels, at the moment one feels it, that is a marvellous thing. I have never seen this anywhere before; though in a Jewish family one approximates to it at times.

Am accosted, for the third time in two days, by a handsome young man. The same tale on each occasion: he wants to exchange names, do I come from England, will I teach him English? He hopes to emigrate to England or the USA. Sexual? I am not accommodating.

Muse on Cyril Connolly's review in the *Sunday Times* of a new book by Koestler and others about coincidence and the relation between the living and non-living components of the universe. A fascinating piece. It seems that a machine designed to select random numbers, of which some do and some do not operate to provide food and warmth to a cageful of animals, will release more operant numbers when the cage is full of cold and hungry creatures than when it is empty; i.e. there is a psychokinetic effect mediated by the animals' needs. Now, from their point of view, the machine is Deity, dispensing their essential requirements according to their prayers. In the beginning, the Universe created God!

Sitting in the hotel garden on this free afternoon, the sun is so hot that I have to seek shade under the trees. And it is well on in November!

Stroll through the streets, across a dry river bed – the Rudkhaneh

E Khosk – between the northern limits of Shiraz proper to the foot
of the mountains. Beyond are new housing districts. Also a fascinating
street-market, not so different from street-markets anywhere, give and
take some points of detail, but nostalgic for me because it recalls the
High Street market stalls of the East End suburb where I was a child,
the naphtha flares in the evening, the stir and excitement. But here
there are nuts of all kinds, some unknown spices, pomegranates, fresh
amber-coloured dates, trays of sheep-hearts, rice and meat-stew for
eating on the spot, green melons that resemble marrows, fruits I can't
name, seeds, great trays of baby beets boiled and eaten with butter.
And people. On the northern outskirts, the tomb of Hafiz, poet and
meditator:

> Thou who didst dwell where Ruknabad once ran
> Melodious beneath the Persian sky
> And watch with mind serene and steady eye
> The tragic play that is the life of man;
> And, seeing it was so since earth began
> And shall continue after thou and I,
> Being spent as swiftly as a lover's sigh,
> Depart upon Death's trackless caravan;
> Out of dross sound by sovereign alchemy
> Didst fashion melodies of liquid gold,
> Creating riches of thy penury,
> Transmuting Death to immortality;
> Accept these words that leave the whole untold,
> And in fresh youth renew thy wisdom old.*

It is cool here, withdrawn, a place of peace – water, marble columns,
blood-red flowers, the mountains behind. A holy place, like the Ktab
Minah in Delhi, or like Glastonbury.

Friday 9 November. The Christian Hospital. Well-built, cool, solid,
the nearest approach to an English hospital so far. Impressed with the
care and cleanliness and the staff, English and Shirazi. A coincidence:
a rubber bandage essential for an operation tomorrow, the absence of
which has been plaguing me, turns up in the physiotherapy depart-

---

* From *Fifty Poems of Hafiz,* transl. Arthur J. Arberry. Cambridge University Press, 1947.

ment. The Lord, in my experience, *always* provides. The treatment is efficient, patients without resources are not charged; but there is a price for this on the evangelical side. I feel they should be content to serve the people freely and devotedly as professed Christians and leave it to the locals to enquire the nature of the force that impels them. (This may seem unkind. But one recalls a remark by the Bishop of Stepney, in 1896, when consecrating a medical mission to the Jews: 'Sick people are more susceptible to spiritual influences, and the knowledge put into their minds at such a time may afterwards lead to good results.') I am shown a four-months-old child with bilateral congenital dislocation of the hips, and am informed that she could not be seen without fee at the other hospitals, or not for several months, and the Mission Hospital has no orthopaedic service, and will I treat her at one of the other hospitals where I am attached? I am furious and I will. Every day counts in this condition, for if the head of the femur is left displaced, the hip socket will increasingly fail to accommodate to it and reduction becomes more difficult, and therefore more dangerous.

My feelings about charges are mixed. Here in Iran nearly everyone has to pay for nearly everything. Patients are charged for drugs, tests, visits, plaster-casts according to size, blood transfusions. Blood donors are scarce; so students and their relatives are induced, or bribed, to give blood by gifts of textbooks and instruments, value proportionate to volume given. One's first reaction to this might well be one of revulsion. But let me elaborate on the question of patient payment, the free National Health Service – free at the time of use, though paid for out of income-tax and contributions – versus the pay system of the United States, the abuse of a free service versus the suffering of those who cannot afford to pay.

When I was young and enthusiastic, I was an advocate of a free NHS at a time when a doctor who said so gained instant unpopularity. After I became a consultant in 1946, two years before the 'appointed day' of Nye Bevan, my feelings began to change. At that time, married with several children, I received no payment whatever outside my private fees. But the consultants had a proprietorial interest in and an identification with the hospital, the lay administrators were submissive and stood to attention – how prehistoric that now seems, when the boot is on the other foot! – and the patients were grateful. Were they then under-treated? I am sure of this: not a single patient with a life-threatening emergency who is saved now would not have been saved before 1948, making allowances for certain technical advances. A medical empire, a National Disease Service, has certainly been created; and if one thing is certain, it is that in medicine supply creates demand. To put it another way: surgery abhors a vacuum, and we must remember that the NHS brought, for the first time, young, enthusiastic and technically well-qualified surgeons to virgin territories. In orthopaedics, as in other fields, there is no – literally no – limit to technical developments. We once had our hands full with accidents, poliomyelitis and skeletal tuberculosis; and then people put up with, and grumbled about, their chronic arthritis as an inevitable part of life. Now polio and tuberculosis are extinct in Britain and time and energy are free for new treatments of osteoarthritis, the development of biological engineering, the total mechanical replacement of arthritic joints. It is probably a false evolution, since it is basically contemptuous of biological considerations, which it supplants. But, when it has eventually been mastered, other fields, now considered impracticable, will beckon. And none of this is linked to national needs. At the point of consultation a doctor is always faced with an individual and his problems; but when overall resources are inadequate for all requirements – and they will always be as medicine develops – some priorities must be laid down that attempt to reconcile what is needed for the individual with what the nation can afford to supply and with the very tricky – and basically insoluble – question as to which patients are most worth salvaging from the viewpoint of the national economy. These questions are heart-searching; and, to give due credit to the administration of the NHS, there has never, as far as I know, been any official interference with clinical freedom to decide in these matters – except, possibly, in the matter of heart transplants.

Now, where payment for treatment is concerned, it could never be other than disproportionate to the time and skill and technical expertise required, except in the field of full-scale private practice. What then is to be done? My personal hero, Hugh Owen Thomas, the founder of orthopaedic surgery in Britain, a fanatical overworker and perfectionist, insisted that every patient, however poor, should pay something, however little, to salvage his own self-respect and to make him value his treatment. (Thomas often immediately returned the payment, and more, in kind in the form of free meals.) I think it is right that patients should have to put their hands in their pockets at the time of treatment, because it makes them realize that heavy costs are involved, even if they subsequently get most or all of the charge back from a governmental or private insurance scheme. I would say: from each patient according to his ability to pay, to each according to his medical needs; a medical equivalent of a famous Marxist aphorism.

As to rights and entitlements: I do not believe that in this utterly non-human universe there is anyone above to dispense rights or other goodies. If there is any motto I would like to see permanently emblazoned in the skies over our country, it is 'No one is entitled to anything!', whether it is life, liberty, the pursuit of happiness, wealth, health, education or housing. Everything is fortuitous; we are lucky to survive. But I have some reservations, for if one considers a child in its home and family setting it would obviously say, if it could assess the problem, that it *was* entitled to father and mother, food and security, that these things *are* given. And there are the moments we all know, when we experience what Freud called the 'oceanic feeling', when we know that we have a place in the universe and that it is our home. Either he was right, and it is a mystic sense of union with the breast, or it means something that entirely contradicts what I know, intellectually, to be true. I feel more and more uncertain about the answer the older I get.

In the hotel bar a British ex-army officer tells how he was captured at Arnhem, of how he was tortured, his left thumb cut off, his head held immersed in a bucket of water, how they pretended to shoot him, to make him reveal military dispositions. He lost, he says, the capacity to be afraid after a time. But he does not seem to hate the Germans, rather the Dutch traitors – and there were some – who helped them. Anyway, he lived to see his tormentor executed, after Nuremberg. He added that in Greece, during the civil war following the German collapse, communist prisoners were tied back-to-back, drenched in petrol and set on fire in the streets of Salonika, after which the British handed over no further prisoners to their Greek government allies. I admire this brave modest man, who has given a lifetime of hard and dangerous service to his country, and think of his standing *vis-à-vis* the sort of left-wing intellectuals I once used to consort with. They would affect to despise him and he is worth a hundred of any one of them. His aphorism that men govern a country best when they have a direct financial stake in its prosperity appeals to me, a one-time Labour voter who now has to support the Conservatives as the party likely to do the country least harm. I feel increasingly that government has become too serious a matter to be left to the politicians, and that the major need of our time is increasingly to depoliticize the management of the nation-state and international affairs. Once objectives are agreed and defined – and admittedly this is largely a political matter – there is surely only one best way to achieve these aims with the greatest good for the greatest number, and this is a matter for managers and experts and scientists. I would rather have Beeching or Robens at the head of affairs than any party Prime Minister; and it is no use arguing that the Civil Service or other expert advisers perform the functions concerned, because, however efficient and objective they may be, they are always subject to overriding and often irrational decisions from the top. No one would attempt to manage on political lines a large and complex industrial organization, and that is exactly what modern Britain is. Political considerations are becoming increasingly irrelevant, and more and more of the public know this instinctively and desperately want to be rid of the whole box of tricks.

Drinks in the garden in the dusk with a *New York Times* man and his wife; I think, as so often, how nice nice Americans are.

Saturday 10 November. Play myself in. At 7.30 a tendon transplant operation on a lad of twenty. This has been weighing on my mind for some days but, as usual after preliminary worrying, goes very smoothly and possibly made some impression on the local talent. At any rate, I feel much better afterwards. Why these obsessional anticipatory worries, useless, nagging? An analyst might say – has said – that the fear is not so much that one will not be able to perform, but that one *will* be able, and so become exposed to increasing and persistent demands. If one's basic attitude is 'See how helpless I am!', this is so inconsistent with being an efficient executive in surgery or any other field as to make work go against the grain and create unnecessary exhaustion. Do mature persons suffer from obsessions?

While relaxing from this minor procedure, an urgent telephone call from the Nemazee. My curly-haired girl is worse, legs not working, bladder going. I rush across and decide to operate this morning, instead of Monday as scheduled. It goes well – for me. For her, there is a malignant growth springing from a lumbar vertebra, exploding into the superficial muscles, growing into the spinal canal to compress the cord. I do an extensive decompression, but the main focus of the lesion is out of reach and irremovable. All this is done in a gay and elevated, rather brittle mood, and I discuss the case and the hopeless prognosis lightly with the residents. I suppose I am as divorced from my true feelings about this child as the mourning woman on the pavement was identified with hers. No matter, it will catch up with me, it always does.

Later. About to do my faculty duties and attend a chest conference – about which I know nothing – when I am whisked away by a delightful Austrian professor of pathology who shows me the Asian Institute and the old harem instead.

11 November. The child is not doing too badly – I am always surprised to find my patients alive the next day – but has some weakness of the legs. The parents resist accepting that she has a tumour. On the ward round, cases of infection and tuberculosis of bone such as we never see at home, and so severe that my opinion has to be based on general principles rather than personal experience. If there is no student or resident available to interpret, I can't talk to these patients, my approach has to be veterinary. I am asked to see a girl who has been admitted near death with suppuration in the pericardial sac round the heart. They have done a magnificent job in saving her life; my concern is with a relatively minor aspect, the spread of infection to one knee. She is a tall, magnificent creature from one of the villages or tribes, raven-haired with thick strokes of eyebrows. I would put her at twenty-one or twenty-two, but she is only fifteen; everyone here looks older than their years and the expectation of life is less than ours. She is desperately ill, with dry sores on her lips, and any attempt to move the knee elicits repeated wailings that sound very like the '*Oi veh*!' familiar to me as a child. We give her a large shot of sedative and I put her leg in plaster. The nurses do not bother to help, there are no screens round the bed, and the scene is watched by the other patients and a visiting electrician. One's impression is that these patients feel it their duty to express their symptoms forcibly to establish their claim to be ill; they do not suffer in silence. This again I recognize from a Jewish upbringing. Incidentally, I am depressed by the general absence of nurses from the wards. As in the States, they preside graciously at the nursing station, which is a good way away down the corridor. The patients are out of sight, and there is a general lack of compassion. A girl as sick as this at home would have a nurse by her side most of the time; instead the child is wide awake, and terrified, and quite alone.

Nothing happens here on time. For any appointment or arrangement one must mentally add fifteen to thirty minutes to the stated time. I get into the habit of carrying my translation work around with me to fill in the waiting periods usefully. No lunch today as all this rice is putting weight on; instead, iced pomegranate juice in the sun – one of the most delicious drinks I have ever tasted.

The Shah arrives in Shiraz today. His portrait is everywhere. He does a magnificent job in governing this large, potentially wealthy, rather unruly and individualistic country, which would fall to pieces and succumb to corruption without his firm drive. I wish. . . .

12 November. Arrive to operate at 7.15, but can't get started till nearly 9. It is explained that, because of the Shah's visit, one of the operating theatres has to be kept in permanent readiness, in case of accident or assassination, I suppose. Blood too. Of course, this is routine where heads of state are concerned. My patient is a policeman with a torn knee cartilage; this is very rare in Iran and they are impressed with my rapidity – fifteen minutes instead of the hour they'd expected.

I muse on the universal coverage we have for orthopaedic care in England, and indeed for all other fields of medicine and surgery. There is no county, no corner of the British Isles where the population does not have reasonably early and easy access to a well-trained specialist, without payment. It was not always so; before 1948 large areas, even in London itself, had no such cover, and patients had to visit the great teaching hospitals. Seen from today, the situation would seem to have been unbearable; but as people do not miss what they do not know, what we would now regard as periods of desperate deprivation in history were not felt as such because the knowledge of the *possibility* of anything better did not exist. Happiness, and despair and discontent, are all in the mind, and only in the mind. What is intolerable is awareness that better standards exist, are available to others but not to oneself.

Of course, we still have the barrier of the waiting-list, but not for urgent cases; here, in Shiraz, I have seen or heard of children with congenital deformities or life-threatening bone infections being turned away. The situation is roughly on a par with that of England in the early twentieth century; the knowledge exists but is not disseminated, not generally available. What is needed in Iran is what developed to meet this challenge at home: great pioneers like Robert Jones and Agnes Hunt to found the first orthopaedic hospitals, to set up peripheral clinics to locate and gather in the sick. The doctors here don't much want to go out into the villages; urban practice is far more exciting and rewarding. But what matters is how things are developing, and the hopeful fact is that something is now being done to organize expert teams to go out into the villages.

Evening, a British Council soirée. Doctors, British tank-men on loan to show the locals how to use the hardware we sell them, a WHO water-engineer from Boston, Shirazi notabilities. I have always felt that these international organizations – the British Council, WHO and similar bodies, the Foreign Service and international civil servants – stand in an elevated position, outside the trials and tribulations of real life, intent on esoteric problems and intrigues, conditions of service, home leave and pensions. I reflect on my own service with WHO, how unreal it all was, to be suddenly translated from suburban surgery to the shores of Lake Leman. How much good WHO as a whole does, is not for me to say, and I lack the knowledge to do so; but as an editor of the WHO *Chronicle* I did, in fact, have to record the achievements and exploits of this body. At that time, it was very lopsided. The existence of nearly a thousand million people in China was no more taken into account than the weather in Southern Ireland in a BBC weather report. Because of the fear of offending Catholic member states, no reference to population problems or contraception was allowed in any publication. The position has now completely changed in both respects. There have been some striking successes, for instance with regard to the campaign against smallpox. The fact that this and so many other health problems can be dealt with on a global scale, for the first time in history, evokes the vision of H. G. Wells that the peace of the world might slowly evolve from the international organizations that emerged from the war.

And yet. . . . I suppose there is always a wretched contrast between what people do, or aim to do, and how they behave and talk about it. Anyone who has had the opportunity of eavesdropping on surgical gossip in a changing-room would find it difficult to understand how such frivolous, cynical, heartless monsters could do the work they are actually seen to do. The same must apply to the professional shop of lawyers, politicians, actors: cynicism, carping criticism, self-denigration, even the affectation of the utter worthlessness of their activities, are merely the other face of devotion, self-sacrifice, real humility. What is one to do or say, after four hours of desperately intense and demanding work trying to fit together the pieces of a terribly injured motorcyclist – and some of the pieces are literally missing, sometimes brought along by the police from the gutter – except to light a cigarette and say: 'What a bloody waste of time! Stupid bastard, he was asking for it!' Similarly, in WHO there was an enormous gap between the pieties prated by the Director-General at the annual Assembly and the lazy inertia and malicious gossip prevalent in the offices of that institution. Everything was carried out at a slow pace; in the vast corridors of the Palais des Nations physical progress was so retarded that it came to be known as the Palais Glide. And the verbiage! Over and over again what I wrote had to be rewritten many times to satisfy the formal, fussy requirements of some South American or African superior who did not hesitate to instruct me in the syntax and punctuation of the English language. Certain words were sacrosanct: one of these, 'prevention', enabled me to make one of my few good jokes. At a solemn weekly staff meeting, the sort of meeting at which Americans use the word 'data' in the singular, an elevated person was talking about primary prevention – stopping disease from ever beginning; secondary prevention – the treatment of established disease and restoration to normal; and tertiary prevention – the arrest of disease, though without actual reversal and cure. As he emphasized these points with waves of a stubby finger and gleams through thick glasses, I could not resist saying: 'But you have forgotten to mention quarternary prevention.' 'Quarternary prevention, what's that?' 'Why, sir, resurrection!' This did *not* go down well.

I like to be used, and to be useful, and it soon became clear that this was not possible in Geneva, though the actual editorial work, like all technical work, had its own demanding requirements and standards of excellence. So I settled to leave at the end of a year, not without having first developed an acute gastric ulcer. When I returned to the hospital, after not having seen a patient or handled a scalpel for twelve months, I seriously wondered what on earth was going to happen at my first operating list. I had no idea whatever. But worries

were needless; things went as well as if I had been away for only a
week. Surgery is like sex or riding a bicycle, you never lose the knack,
although a break of two or three years *would* make a difference.

13 November. My policeman is making the most of his operation.
Writhing in alleged agony, perspiring, complaining excessively. In
fact, he is doing well. He kisses my hand, prays that the sun may shine
on me forever. My little girl and her parents are all smiles today. She
feels much better, can move her legs, there is a general atmosphere of
hopefulness and recovery which infects even me, the more so as one is
professionally attuned to a cheerful, somewhat bullying attitude as
one urges patients back to normality. Can't bring myself to destroy all
this with the harsh truth; time will do that soon enough.

The students are keen, but do not appear anxious to be made to
think. 'Please tell us the important facts clearly so that we may write
them down' is what they actually say, and the book is mightier than
the bedside. Clinical teaching (*cline* = a bed) is less important than a
chapter-heading.

Persepolis. I enjoy the immense satisfaction of being personally con-
ducted round these magnificent ruins by Professor Dutz, a pathologist
at the hospital who is also no mean archaeologist and has written the
standard work on the subject. Thirty minutes from Shiraz along a
road traversing wild and beautiful mountain scenery. I do not feel
capable of adequately describing Persepolis at this stage; it needs to be
visited over and over again, like the Taj Mahal. There are certain
difficulties. It is all highly organized, with guides and tape-recorded
programmes, a museum and a splendid hotel nearby, together with
the Shah's magnificent tent-city erected for the anniversary celebra-
tions of the Persian Empire a few years back. All this seems to prevent
one from coming to grips with the antiquities; one would like to be
alone on this platform overlooking the vast plain, with the great
columns rising to the sky. And the reliefs, the figures look so fresh and
sharp, it is hard to believe that they are presented to us across a gap
of two thousand years. We spend hours on the site, clambering over
the rocks to reach the ancient tombs in the cliff face. Drive back in the
dark – very dangerous as every approaching driver blinks his head-
lights on and off – the flaring jet of burning gas from the new refinery,
home to Shiraz under the Koran Gate. Am being taken by other

friends in a few days. But I am not overwhelmed by Persepolis as one is by the Taj, which is always better than one expects. Rather, I am fascinated by what Persepolis once *was*.

14 November. Exasperation and exhaustion in the outpatient clinic. No one on time; arrive at 8 a.m., do not get off the ground till 9.15. Patients arrive accompanied by their families, fathers bring their sons of forty! My little girl flourishes, the policeman is in hysterical collapse. Afternoon seminar: the students are like young birds waiting to be fed with dogmatic statements to be written down. But active thinking, no! Long, long police forms to be filled and photographs to be supplied for work and residence permits. I learn later that these serve no purpose whatever and disregard future requests. Tonight, the equivalent of a fine English June evening, the Shirazis complain bitterly of the cold and turn on their electric fires. I read of the state of emergency in the UK, imminent petrol-rationing, strikes, am worried about my wife and family facing difficulties of transport, heating and lighting, and about the deteriorating value of my travellers' cheques, in that order. Particularly worried as there is no word from home, after seventeen days. From here England is a soggy little island, deprived of sunlight, rent by political dissension, and heading for the economic rocks.

15 November. Seminar at seven, so rise in the half-light, mountains looming grey and aweful. This time I pull out all the stops, give them a review of my experience of hip surgery over twenty-five years, with a gratifying response. A lazy day afterwards; afternoon stroll through the crowded quarters and the bazaar. The Iran Crafts centre and a magnificent old caravanserai turned into a tea-house flank a delightful little square with a pool and orange trees.

Have been immersed in reading in my extensive spare time, mainly *Salammbô*, now finished. An amazing and absorbing recreation of Carthage. How did Flaubert gather all this apparently authentic detail, in some ways resembling Scott in this respect? And how can the same man have written *Madame Bovary*? I begin on Livy's *Wars Against Hannibal* without a pause.

16 November. Plethoric and depressed from overeating, I plan to work in the hotel garden all day, editing the proceedings of an orthopaedic congress for a Dutch academic institution. Decline an invitation to a picnic at Persepolis with Dr Dutz and the Director of the British Council, but am finally dragged off on this excursion by another invitee, a young physician on secondment from St Thomas's Hospital in London. The picnic is high up in a fold of the mountains behind Persepolis. We find, casually, inscriptions on the cave walls thousands of years old. Before us spreads a vast plain ringed round by mountains. We pass a cubical mass of stone on which the Zoroastrians used to lay their dead to be picked clean by vultures, the earth being too hard to dig, fire too sacred; later their bones were interred in pockets in the hillside. There is a trough on top of the stone the size of a man, and smaller troughs for children and animals. Dutz, careering too fast across the stony countryside, fractures the sump of his Mercedes. The remainder of the afternoon is spent at various garages doing makeshift repairs with chewing-gum, dates, and a piece of wood wrapped in rags. Anywhere else this would have been maddeningly irritating. Here, in the clear golden sunlight and the relaxed atmosphere of an Iranian Friday afternoon, it seems a pleasant way of passing the time.

17 November. Exasperation reaches a peak. I discover, quite by chance, that a young woman has been admitted under my care to have a bone-graft for an ununited fracture of the tibia. No one has bothered to tell me, there is no evidence that the interne has seen the patient, nothing has been done and the patient is paying a high daily rate for all this neglect. I fume, and am baffled by this damned language barrier that prevents me from communicating directly with the girl and the nurse. The girl with the pericardial infection is not in her bed, dead I presume, but am unable to obtain any confirmation from anyone – nurses, patients or the house physician.

I see now that I have a serious problem on my hands: chronic underwork of such a degree as to be seriously frustrating, and a gross lack of social contacts. As regards the former, I have fortunately brought with me a mass of translation work, which might as well be done in the Medical School Library as elsewhere; and my old friends, Excerpta Medica of Amsterdam, who are in the habit of sending me editorial work wherever in the world I happen to be, have turned up trumps again. In fact, they are the only people who have yet written to me!

As for the social aspect, I don't mind it too much as I am essentially a rather solitary person and normally so fragmented by the demands of innumerable patients and a large family that it is a pleasure to find myself reintegrated and enjoying a good relationship with myself, which I had thought lost long since. But it will be dangerous to let it go too far. Even casual contacts are helpful, and I find myself seeking them out. In the bar I chat with a titanic German widow of over sixty who is on a prolonged tour, driving alone all over Turkey and Iran. I suppose the purpose – one purpose – of other people is to reflect oneself, to provide the evidence that one is really there, alive and communicating. It is better than Narcissus's pool.

Of course, the best way to overcome loneliness – and to learn Farsi – would be to have an affair. There is some evidence that this would not be difficult, though there might always be complications and tedium, and I do not really want to be unfaithful. Also, I am getting too old for this kind of thing.

To choose a partner who does not speak English is perhaps also one of the secrets of a happy marriage. It takes that much longer to discover how bored one is.

18 November. Mounting irritation at not being as fully and usefully employed as I should like to be. Decide to attempt to cut my stay short by a few weeks and, having taken this decision, feel much better. All, no doubt, based on a long-standing neurotic unwillingness to go on to the end of anything, to see the last patient, to fulfil the very last appointment. Of course, as the analysts would say, we all know what that last appointment is, and why cancelling it gives so much pleasure.

Try to ring my wife and am told that communications are interrupted for fifteen days; nevertheless, am connected at three in the morning. Such pleasure to make this contact, to feel that my home base is intact. We agree that I shall try to shorten my contract.

19 November. A letter from Margaret Crosland, the distinguished writer and translator, authority on Cocteau and Colette. Margaret, who lives in the next village to mine in Sussex, first enrolled me in the translation racket. Since then we have turned translating Colette, and much other work besides, into a cottage industry.

I find translation exacting, teasing, immensely stimulating intellectually and very rewarding – though I don't mean financially, or even professionally. For it remains as true as when Belloc gave his Taylorian Lecture on the subject in 1931 that translation, though a subsidiary art, is an important and difficult one which attracts little pay and less celebrity. Or, to adapt Johnson's epigram on lexicographers – who are, after all, only translators of another kind – 'Every other author may aspire to praise; the translator can only hope to escape reproach.'

The first and permanent difficulty about translation is that it is basically impossible. As Tolstoy said, a translation is like looking at the wrong side of the carpet. One gets a fair general idea of the pattern, but it is nothing like the right side. There are no exact equivalents; a word in one language does not mean precisely the same as the corresponding word in another, and if it seems to, the associations it excites will differ in different social settings. And I am referring here to traps far more subtle than our old friends, the *faux amis: déception,* which does not mean deception, but disappointment; *fastidieux,* which means not fastidious but bloody boring, as in washing-up.

The translator must translate into his own language, and that he must know very well indeed. But, short of translating *à coups de dictionnaire,* he need not know perfectly the language he is translating from. In fact, the better he knows it, the worse the translation, until we reach the perfect bilingual, who cannot translate at all. Hence the paradox that, often, we can read and understand and thoroughly enjoy a book in a foreign language and yet find it hellishly difficult to translate. There must be an urge to render the original material into a form understandable to one's fellow-countrymen. And what is the source of this urge if not one's own imperfect understanding? We interpret to ourselves before interpreting to others. Belloc raises the point, fascinating but one I am not competent to pronounce on, whether one does not translate first into a basic, unspoken Ur-language, and from that into English. It is certain, at any rate for a predominantly visual thinker, that when one recalls a book one has read in the past, it is not in terms of language.

The actual process of translation I always think of as an invasion. It must begin with a thorough study of the enemy in depth; the foreign text must be read *in toto* before committing a word to paper. Then the translation must advance through it in a steady wave, flowing round and leaving behind any resistant strongpoints to be returned to and reduced later, when the unconscious has done its work, often overnight. The translation must generally be pretty faithful to the original, but not too faithful; the translator should not hesitate to depart, or even to improvise, if it helps to convey the flavour of the original. This is particularly so with a language as concise as Latin. Here is an example. Catullus wrote a poem bewailing Lesbia's infidelity, a sort of contemporary 'I wonder who's kissing her now'. Here is part of this sad little piece:

> *Quis nunc te adibit? cui videberis bella?*
> *quem nunc amabis? cujus esse diceris?*
> *quem basiabis? cui labella mordebis?*

Stuttaford renders this as follows: 'Who now will seek you out? Whom will your charms inflame? Whom will you love? Whose then will you be called? Whom will you kiss? Whose lips will you bite in amorous frenzy?'

Now there is nothing whatever about 'amorous frenzy' in the original. It is pure invention. But it is perfect.

Finish Livy on Hannibal. It reads like a novel, largely due, no doubt, to Aubrey de Selincourt's splendid translation. One or two points stand out. First, as also made so clear in *Salammbô,* the very *personal* nature of ancient warfare. It was mostly hand-to-hand; and even in cavalry actions you selected your opponent and went for him. There was nothing at a distance, none of your modern impersonal slaughter, if we exclude the elephants and the *ballistae* used to sling missiles over a city wall. Second, the tremendous *resilience* of Rome, and her adherence to the proper religious rites and forms of government under the most terrible stresses. When the campagna before the city was devastated, and Hannibal's army at the very gates, a Roman army left by another gate on the way to reinforce the armies in Sicily! That is sublime. And those decades of conflict between Rome and Carthage: how futile they seem in retrospect, how urgent at the time. The polarization of the known world between these two super-powers, the struggle *à outrance,* how reminiscent of today, how sure we are that, if universal destruction had been the necessary condition of victory, that is what they would have chosen. Literally, nothing changes. Whether it is the Peloponnesian War, the Thirty Years' War, or any of our more recent struggles, it is only too clear that history teaches us that history teaches us nothing. Old passions and new weapons – that is the description of our state today.

20 November. Having decided to cut this tour of duty short, if the administrators here and in London agree, I am revivified by a long and busy day. At 7.30 – and on time for a change – a bone-grafting operation for the young woman with the ununited fracture of the tibia. All goes reasonably well, though not perfectly for lack of certain instruments. Find myself irritable in the theatre and tending to shout a bit at the staff. A splendid lunch in the hospital canteen – delicious rice and lamb stew with yoghourt.

A long outpatient clinic in the afternoon. First, a wealthy young married woman who has come down from Teheran with her daughter to see me. (It emerges during the afternoon that the news has spread that there is a new doctor in town, and a number of orthopaedic wrecks, and neurotics, have decided to try their luck.) This woman complains of diffuse aches and pains in the back and legs. She has been everywhere for a cure. She is obviously depressive, without having to be interpreted, and questions reveal that she is unhappy, finds every day an ordeal and life not worth living. But it is difficult to convince her that her symptoms are psychogenic. It always is. Yet depression often presents for the early months with just such somatic and hypo-chondriacal symptoms. This is so-called 'masked' depression; and it causes a lot of waste of time and trouble for those general practitioners who do not, for a time, realize that the leading features conceal and overlie a spiritual sickness. They are a call for help, indicate that the sufferer has come to the end of the road; if they are misinterpreted, or ignored, there is always suicide.

I have myself a considerable personal experience of depression, use-lessly and wastefully treated by psychoanalysis. So I know what this particular hell is like, and from the inside. My student-interpreter says cynically: 'In Iran we find the best treatment for this type of case is lots of investigations, lots of X-rays, different kinds of drugs, etc.' I ask him to tell her that I don't intend to waste her and my time and her money on further useless investigations, that her trouble is basically depressive, that it is very real, and that she must have psychiatric treat-ment. I say this as much to myself as to her; there is always the ten-dency, in such cases, to feel that one has unmasked a pretender, that if it is not organic disease it can be ignored, contemptuously even. This attitude – which is one that I regret to say I absorbed with contemporary medical students before the war – is, I hope, now dying out. Yet there is always the innate tendency to regard only organic disease as virtuous, and psychological disturbance masked by somatic symptoms as the sign of an impostor – fraudulent manifestations to be unmasked as one might unmask a fraudulent medium. People so often say: 'It's all in the mind', and yet it is only what we feel that matters in this life. The facts are relatively unimportant; it is what we feel about them that counts, which is why I have always resisted when analysts have tried to ram the importance of facts down my throat. If a man thinks he is ill, he *is* ill; if he is happy, he *is* happy, though he may be dying of cancer. It seems to me that depression is essentially the expression of a soul sick for lack of fulfilment, life's progress inexorably blocked. We may not know what it is we want; but that does not prevent us from suffering for lack of it, from searching with increasing desperation for the answer to the dread question: 'What shall I do to be saved?'

The woman's daughter, aged fourteen, does have a serious physical problem; and, as so often in such cases, is not at all perturbed. Illness as justification. She has been treated for congenital dislocation of the hip by several authorities, including an eminent English surgeon. The result is terrible and something else will have to be done before long. The operation required – total replacement of the joint with a metal and plastic substitute – cannot be done in this country, and I tell the mother to bring her daughter to see me in London next year.

A woman of twenty-six, in multicoloured garments, up from Bandar Abbas. She has a severe limp. She fell down a well a year ago and has had some desultory treatment from the local practitioners. The X-ray shows a fracture of the neck of the femur; the hip is disorganized. This is a difficult problem as it is impossible now to mend the fracture. Decide to admit her for replacement of the damaged part with a metal insert – the best we can do here, but really the second-best. As she leaves she turns to address a last remark through the interpreter. He tells me: 'She says that her husband has told her he will divorce her if you are unable to cure her.'

The result of all this work – minor by English standards – is that I feel much more valid. I need my patients at least as much as they need me: they make me feel replenished, rewarded, enriched – and this is hardly in pecuniary terms! This is something of a problem at home, since the work I need to maintain my self-respect leaves me too

exhausted at evenings and weekends to devote proper attention to my
family, who get the dog-ends and leavings from my professional commitment. I don't know the answer to this; retirement certainly won't
help. There is no fixed retiring age in Iran, so perhaps one could come
out here with one's pension and continue working at this relaxed
pace. . . .

The hotel bar is full of American communications engineers,
Danish oil-pipe layers, German and French tourists. The talk is mainly
of company frustrations.

21 November. I begin to understand how easy it would be to succumb
to the local tempo. I suppose I must be Asiatic in origin but am
thoroughly imbued with the Nordic temperament, the need to work
to justify one's existence to God. If one did retire to a place like this,
or to the French countryside, it would take a year or two to become
thoroughly adapted.

Go for a long walk to the very edge of town, to Saadi's tomb. Walking here is like walking in Switzerland. One is six thousand feet up, the
clear, brilliant light is intoxicating, one feels weightless, distances
crumble, the old feel young. Saadi was a great mystic, prophet and
healer; the hospital is named after him. The tomb is a simple and
beautiful structure of alabaster. Much of oriental building I find
tawdry; but here there is great simplicity and elegance and a particular pleasure in the tiled walls of the shrine, which depict roses, irises
and birds. Back at the hotel in time to see the sun sink behind the
mountains to the south, a moment of *cafard*, thoughts of the first drink
of the evening. But there is another party at the University Club
tonight – the hospital consultants are taking it in turns to entertain
each other.

Progress: parking meters have just been installed on Darius Avenue.

Begin Michael Holroyd's *Lytton Strachey*. From the first words of
the introduction it is clear that the book will be a delight.

22 November. My child with the dislocated hips has not yet been
admitted. As the mother brought him to my clinic a week ago, and as I
had then asked the house-surgeon to see to the matter forthwith, I
cross-examine him:

'Why wasn't that child I spoke to you about admitted on Monday?'

'There were no beds available. It was impossible.'

'And today?'

'Oh, we have plenty of beds today.'

'Then why isn't the child in hospital?'

'They were not here today, so I could do nothing.'

It is clear that he expects the mother and child to appear daily at the hospital gates, supplicants for admission, until they hit on a lucky day.

'But you have the address on the outpatient notes. Can't you send for them?'

A look of bewilderment:

'Oh no, we can't do that. That is not done here!'

And, in fact, it is not done to notify patients by letter or telephone that a bed is available. It is my turn to be baffled; there is no more I can do. The child is not admitted, the days pass, the chances of cure slip away.

On the whole, beggars are few here; and those there are are not importunate. But I do object to the type who holds a child on his lap, often late at night when the child is asleep and, I suspect, hired out for the purpose, exhibiting its deformed limbs to the public gaze.

People will patiently suffer the most terrible burdens, of the flesh or the spirit, which they immediately find intolerable if the faintest hope of relief appears. If someone discovers a possible cure for death, how we shall rage and rail for it and how weighted and shadowed our previous lives will seem to have been.

The Shah Ceragh. A vast complex of mosques, mirrored halls and theological seminary. Two stupendous multicoloured domes. Half the population of Shiraz seems to be strolling and chatting here in the relaxed weekend atmosphere of Thursday afternoon. Having read in a guide-book that the seminary is holy ground, I judge it wise to ask the gate-keeper, leaning on a silver baton, whether I may enter – in dumb show. He welcomes me in; but I have taken only a few steps when I am violently assailed from behind and my clothes tugged at. Various possibilities flash through my mind: that I am being frisked for a camera, which I have, or a weapon, or that I should have removed my shoes. But it is the smiling gate-keeper straightening out my jacket, which has got caught up in my belt.

One difficulty in walking about the secondary streets of Shiraz is the dust raised by the traffic, which settles in lungs and nostrils until it becomes mandatory to find a cup of tea.

Tonight a German quartet. After weeks without music – other than the plaintive Shirazi brand – it is like rain after drought to hear Haydn, Mozart and Beethoven. I had not realized before that Mozart's birth and death dates fell within those of Haydn; he was born later, rose to outshine the other, then fell away and died sooner. What were Haydn's feelings about Mozart's early death? It must all be annotated somewhere.

23 November. The day begins inauspiciously, with Sundayish feelings of uncertainty and gloom. But the sun keeps these away, also the beguilements – and how considerable they are – of *Lytton Strachey.* I provisionally book a flight home for Christmas Eve, though I may not be able to use it. The rest of the day is pure delight. The Chairman of the Department of Surgery, Dr Vaez-Sadeh – a young, handsome, cultured and brilliant surgeon – comes to collect me. We go first to his delightful new house on the northern outskirts of town, right under the mountains, in a precinct where new houses are going up for university members. Then, with the rest of the family, for a picnic at the Agricultural College, a few miles out on the road to Ispahan. This is a splendid institution and, like so many other excellent things in Iran, the brain-child of the Shah. Small bungalows of excellent design are grouped strategically on a slope backed by, and facing, the mountains all around. The occasion is an outing for parents and their children who attend the communal school, an Iranian-American project. We lunch on the grass and then, backs to a warm wall facing a semi-circular amphitheatre of a lawn, are entertained by a village troupe. First, drum (tabla) and an instrument rather like an oboe with a brass disc of a mouthpiece plus reed that makes the sort of noise one hears in a *sardana,* all pleasingly rhythmic and monotonous. Then singing, then a fiddle, all with the drum. Then the hit of the day, a sort of pantomime with a young man, wriggling and dressed in the gorgeous skirts of a village woman, and another dressed as a buffoon and then, literally, as an ass. Then somersaults. The miming is so good that not being able to understand the words is unimportant, as with Punch and Judy. Everyone dances. There are village women, and city girls dressed as village women, and as they gyrate waving a coloured hand-kerchief in each hand, they resemble a flock of butterflies. I have to add that these primitive villagers had remembered to bring a microphone and a loudspeaker.

The day ends splendidly, too. Dr Vaez-Sadeh comes to take me
to the local cabaret. He looks tired and apologizes for being late. He
has just had to operate on a man of forty-five with a malignant
tumour of the liver which was bleeding into the abdominal cavity; he
was unable to save him.

It is a sort of working-man's *café-concert,* with a stage and an enclo-
sure at the back of the hall for women and the middle-class. Tonight
this is occupied by senior members of the medical faculty, all relaxed
and jovial; I assume that none would dare to be seen here singly. The
entertainment is non-stop: violin, drums, a real oboe this time, with
interludes of flute and bagpipes. Every piece sounds the same, the
amplified rhythm is stunning. Young women, quite decorously
dressed, wriggle and hop about the stage or sing plaintively into the
microphone. I am told that they are a great hit with the rich Arabs
who come up here from the Gulf in the summer. The audience claps
in time and now and again a particularly exhilarated individual does
his own solo on the floor of the hall. Chunks of lamb and chicken, flat
bread, a mixture of eggplant and yoghourt and nuts, are laid before
us. This is the way to end a strenuous week.

It has been the happiest day of my stay. The relaxed, friendly
campus atmosphere at the Agricultural College, colleagues meeting
on a day off – in a way like a *kibbutz* atmosphere or that of a social
gathering at a small American university. Far too little of this at home,
partly because of the climate, partly because of the people. No, the
people are the result of the climate, too, and are undone, like everyone else, by sunshine. And in the evening, the visit to the cabaret, to
have the tensions beaten out of one instead of dragging oneself home
to the horrors of television. But this is only possible because Shiraz is
a small city where everyone knows everyone else and nowhere is more
than five minutes from home. I can also picture this kind of evening in
France or Germany, but what have we to offer our visitors at home?
A sordid strip-tease?

24 November. Dysentery heads its ugly rear once more. As if in sympathy, the sky, unsullied this last month, is covered with lowering
clouds. Everything is damp and grey, and the town is suddenly European, French provincial. I drag my carcass to the hospital and experience for the thousandth time that wonderful revivifying experience:

no matter how sick or depressed one may be, this is the place where one *functions*. The patients are, by definition, ill; so, equally by definition, the surgeon must be well. It is the old point about validity; one is what one seems, the hospital *persona* takes over. But a *persona* was only a mask through which the Greek actors spoke. And whether the mask or the entity behind it is the truth, is the perpetually unanswered question of my life, and of many other lives.

Heavy and glutinous after-lunch sleep, intermittently reading admirable Doris Lessing. She must surely be one of our best writers – and I do not refer only to women writers. When I wake, after a healing sleep, great rifts of grey sky are obscuring the mountains to the south, and the muezzin is calling. Struggle down to tea and am buttonholed in the bar by an ancient mariner of an American alcoholic who is recovering from a (pseudo) heart-attack, and explains to me at great length what reality is. But I already know this. It was summed up for me years ago in a *New Yorker* cartoon which showed one of two drunks in a bar looking into the bottom of his glass and saying: 'At last I've discovered what reality is. Reality is what my wife wants!' This is a very profound statement, for it is a woman's function to keep her mate's feet on the ground and restrain his wilder flights of fancy. His function is to roam and stare at the stars while she secures the material conditions of existence and procreation, even if she has to devour him in the process.

A very cosmopolitan party at the Dutzes. They are both pathologists, Austrians, who have worked in the USA and Canada and are about to take off again for the USA after twelve or fifteen years here. Visitors include an Indian pathologist who works in New York and has an Italian wife, and an eminent neurosurgeon from Buenos Aires named Christiansen who is not a Dane, but the descendant of Danes. We are all relaxed and well-intentioned towards each other and the conversation is sparkling; perhaps the best recipe for a successful dinner-party is to have a small group of intelligent persons sharing the same discipline brought together for an hour or two in a strange city, unlikely ever to meet each other again. But the word recipe makes me dwell on the excellence of the dinner itself and of one dish in particular – *fessenjan,* which is chicken cooked with crushed walnuts in concentrated pomegranate juice, and is heavenly.

Oh, and it rained, in torrents, the first rain for six months.

25 November. Summer again, bright and clean, puddles underfoot. An uneventful day.

26 November. Relatively busy. An operation in the morning – only seventy-five minutes late: a man with a hip so seriously infected that I haven't seen its like, I am about to say for twenty years, but in fact ever. This reinforces my moral fibre, which has been wilting lately from lack of employment (whatever is going to happen when I retire?) and from dysentery. It's not as if one said to oneself that only a very privileged few are capable of performing this activity, though this is true enough. I *never* feel this and, whenever congratulated on an operation – which rarely happens as we have no audiences – tend to damp it down and denigrate the whole affair as something anyone could do. Nevertheless, there is sometimes a feeling of solid *worth* which is good to have, and there's also the aspect that surgery can compensate for the lack of many other abilities. A good example is the story told in his memoirs by Ernest Jones, the psychoanalyst, about Wilfred Trotter, the great philosopher-surgeon who was attached to my own school at UCH.

When both were young, before the First German War, Trotter was something of an amateur of psychoanalysis. But he could never really swallow it, it was always above his head, and Jones tells how, when they were both at a European psychoanalytic congress, Trotter became increasingly uncomfortable and embarrassed, perhaps because he recognized even at that early date the spuriousness of these doctrines, which was to become so apparent later, and burst out to Jones: 'Anyway, I'm the only person here who can cut off a leg!' I know exactly how he felt.

In the afternoon another outpatient clinic, small in numbers but expanded to maddening length by delays and longueurs. A child had been brought from Teheran to see me. She had undergone a below-knee amputation for a congenital deformity some years before. I am not clear what is expected of me. The translating student seems to be saying that the parents want me to make a new leg. I look at the father – rich, educated, travelled – and ask again. Yes, he wants to know if I can do some grafting operation and construct a new leg and foot. My fame has indeed spread. For a moment I am almost infected by his credulity, then react strongly and tell him not to waste further time and money seeking impossible operations.

Dinner at the home of the English physiotherapist at the Christian Hospital – a devoted, eager, lonely, woefully tense but *good* man. When I consider his way of life and his isolation in his work, and the way in which he has nevertheless preserved his skill and his keenness, I am humbled. It is cold enough tonight to demand an overcoat for the first time, and before leaving the hotel I had been unwise enough to swallow one of Ali's vodka-limes which, at this altitude, has a sledge-hammer effect that it takes an hour to recover from.

27 November. I have secured my retreat and shall be home for Christmas. Having arranged this, the rest of my stay here begins to be something of an anti-climax. I now see that the ideal arrangement would have been two to four weeks of very high-pressure work, lecturing and operating every day instead of languidly over the week – but this was not in my hands and was not to be. A film this afternoon, at the hospital, showing what is – for Iran – the new operation of total replacement of an arthritic hip-joint with a mechanical articulation. This brilliantly successful procedure is, I am happy to say, of entirely British origin; and, as is so often the case, the Americans, once made a present of the idea, have really gone to town with it with almost Teutonic efficiency. It's the sort of mechanical solution to a biological problem that suits them. The audience here is enthralled and enthusiasts pop up to announce their intention to begin here. I feel it advisable to say a few tempering words. The operation is highly technical; each step must be exactly right; a special operating theatre and theatre team are required, as well as a regular supply of cases. Now osteoarthritis of the hip is as rare in Iran (and in India and Japan) as it is common in Western Europe and the USA; the reasons are not clear – it has something to do with the difference between sitting and squatting and the effects of chronic overweight; and an occasional operation is not going to afford the acquisition of the experience and skill required. One centre for the whole country would seem to be the best arrangement for development of the necessary expertise; otherwise people will have to learn, if they do learn, from their disasters. There is always a stage with a really new and formidable procedure like this, when it can only be done in a few special centres to which other surgeons must make pilgrimage; only later can it spread and become popularized. But the first step is not a technical one, but in the mind: it is the conception of the idea that something can be done to treat what has been the untreatable, to do what has never been imagined before. And this, of course, implies the sort of mental arrogance which is always required when the human race takes a step forward. I well recall, many years ago, a very eminent British orthopaedic surgeon speaking in public of the arrogance – it was his word – of those who thought it might be possible to cure polio. He was a devout Christian. A few months later Salk introduced his vaccine; and now polio is virtually extinct.

28 November. Buy my return ticket to arrive home on Christmas Eve. So the next few weeks will drag.

A seminar in the afternoon. The first forty minutes are occupied by a wrangle between the students and the senior surgeons, who accuse the former of lacking in zeal and application. This goes on at break-neck speed, first in English, then, as tempers rise, lapsing into the vernacular. The situation is an interesting one. The students are not outrageously impolite but answer back as equals without a hint of deference. Out of touch as I may be with the current scene, I can't imagine this confrontation in England. America, yes.

The child with the congenital dislocation of the hip, whom I have been worried about, has been lying untreated in hospital for three days. No one has bothered to tell me. It will be another two or three days before I can find theatre-time for the operation. Altogether a month will have been lost since I first saw him.

Skip a French Cultural Centre concert; my evenings here are much fuller than at home, where I never go out.

29 November. Nemazee. We are shown a terrified boy of nine with an enormous tumour at the knee, a sarcoma of the femur, which shackles him to his bed like a ball and chain. These tumours of children strike terror to the heart of the surgeon; they nearly always constitute a death sentence. Even if treated by immediate amputation, survival is rare; and so, in England, it is commoner to use radiation in the first instance.* I have amputated a leg in a beautiful young working-class girl for a sarcoma of the fibula which was so early that it was hardly visible in the X-ray and my colleagues tried to dissuade me from what

---

* The outlook has improved – somewhat – with recent advances in chemotherapy.

appeared to be a totally unjustified surgical audacity. But she died, nevertheless, within a few months; I am proud that I persuaded her young man to marry her before she did – it gave her a fugitive happiness, him an unspoiled experience of marriage, which is granted to few. *Their* alliance, cut short by death, was not subject to the world's slow stain.

No plans for lunch or the afternoon; but am swept away by Dr Z. to a Rotary lunch at the Kourosh (Cyrus) Hotel, very glamorous and expensive. By far the best cooking so far, an eye-opener: Gulf prawns and rice, a special and scintillating local ice-cream called Paludeh, with embedded grains of sparking starch. After this, despite the blazing sunshine, everything seemed set for an hour in bed; but there was waiting for me at the hotel a personal letter which so destroyed my peace of mind that I went for a long walk instead, to the Koran Gate.

A dinner-party. Many of the guests are American or British army personnel, or civilians instructing the Iranian soldiery to work the complex hardware the West has sold them. The ethics of all this are beyond me. It seems a criminal activity to do this when the Middle East absolutely depends on such importations for its ability to wage war at all. And how is it that, as always, the Americans are so energetic, so undepressed?

30 November. My host of last night sunning himself at my hotel pool with the children while Madame recovers slowly at home. Yet another Persepolis picnic with the proprietor's son and his wife, this time with a group of charming Indians. One of the Indian ladies shows me a new way of tackling a pomegranate – kneading it within its rind so that the segments are fragmented and then piercing a tiny hole to liberate the juice into the mouth. Then to the great new Darius Dam, which is really a reservoir, built with Israeli assistance in mountainous country.

Evening at a Jewish family's Friday night, at the invitation of one of the nurses. The Sabbath is ushered in very much as my father used to do it; but there are some local differences – my host blesses some flowers, the bread is the local flat bread. My mother would recognize the chicken soup and a concoction known in Middle Europe as *tzimmus*. The whole atmosphere is identical with that in which I grew up: the Hebrew service at the beginning of the meal, the general relaxation at the end of a week spent with the Gentiles, the overeating.

Conversation is not as difficult as it might have been since one of the sons is a dental student who speaks with nostalgia of his time in Las Vegas – New Mexico, not Nevada. There are about a hundred thousand Jews in Shiraz and a dozen or so synagogues. There is no ghetto; the Jews are spread over the city. Many have migrated to Israel, from which quite a few return, having found the harsher tempo of work there too much for their native Iranian lethargy. Life in Iran seems to pose no special problems for them, but they do not intermarry as freely as in the West; and they say that if the occasion arises, as during any of the Israel-Arab wars, the poorer Iranians tend to side with their 'Moslem brothers' and express anti-Jewish sentiments, whereas the higher strata of society, and indeed the Shah himself, have a considerable respect for the new expertise Israel has brought to this region. Incidentally, the history of Persian Jewry is very ancient, for it must go back to the First Exile of the sixth century BC. European Jews fall into two great groups: Sephardic or Spanish, and Ashkenazim or Middle European, a division dating from the final Diaspora. The Persian Jews, on the other hand, must have lived continuously in these parts for over 2,500 years.

2 December. I now begin to feel the full frustration of being here, of not being *used.* Now that the original pleasures of this exotic posting have worn off, I am ruefully counting the very considerable financial cost. One can act for the best at the time, but the consequences of one's actions are never to be guaranteed. Unfortunately, to return prematurely to London is going to cause considerable disturbance since the arrangements made for my absence were meant to cover a longer period. Well, one will just have to live through any embarrassments; everything is soon forgotten. There are things in my past life, though, which still make me writhe with embarrassment when I think of them. I can rarely bring myself to speak of them to anyone except, perhaps, to some neutral or therapeutic figure; only to find that my bitter self-condemnation is coolly regarded as altogether excessive. 'That! Only that! Why, we all do that at some time or other!' I am not convinced. What 'that' is, or was, I have no intention of sharing with the reader, except to say that I shall always remain ashamed of certain actions, or inactions, in past years. Strongly-felt emotions are never extinguished. If one was once passionately in love, one always is; the record is stratified and the deeper layers are still there for a digging party to uncover. Still, I am cheered always by Dr Johnson's observation that where there is shame, there may yet be virtue; and by the thought that no condemnation is as keen as self-condemnation. The observer is usually more charitable. I often think of Johnson's account of Savage in his *Lives of the Poets*. Savage behaved, objectively considered, outrageously; he was a scoundrel; but he was a lovable scoundrel and Johnson loved him.

3 December. Yesterday I did an operation on a twenty-year-old boy which did not turn out as I expected. Nothing went wrong, in the sense of a surgical error; and indeed, serious errors of a nature likely to cause disability or threaten life are very uncommon in surgery. But on this occasion, going on the clinical and radiological evidence, I had confidently predicted finding a local disease condition and in the event I was proved wrong. The appearances were normal and I did not achieve what I set out to do. This is bound to happen to any surgeon from time to time, if only because surgery is not mathematics and predictions cannot be made as in the astronomical sense. But whenever it happens to me, I find it infinitely depressing and my morale sags for a few days. There is another factor involved here, however. This emerges when I visit the patient this morning and find him in sparkling form, sitting up and eating his breakfast. We are delighted to see each other and my spirits immediately rise. If I try to analyse the reasons for this they must seem bizarre; but as I know that they are true for me and for some other surgeons too, I shall try to do so. The nervous strain involved in surgical operations varies enormously from surgeon to surgeon, from operation to operation, and in the same surgeon from one time to another. There are times when even major procedures are pure pleasure and exact no spiritual toll; at others I leave the operating theatre more haggard and collapsed than the patient. The next day, as today, seeing one's victim in the ward, alive, well and happy, the relief is so enormous that it can only represent a reaction from the fear that one has mutilated him beyond repair or even murdered him. This may well sound ludicrously fanciful to many of my colleagues; but I have reason to know that others will understand my meaning, and that what is (sometimes) true for me is true for them also. The whole question obviously has deeper implications, connected with the aggressive and destructive impulses that operate at an unconscious level.

Today, because a colleague has gone to Teheran, I have a whole day in the outpatient clinic and feel happy and fulfilled at the end of it. I see some fascinating people and some fascinating conditions, and penetrate beneath those dazzling dresses worn by the village women. Several babies, all looking poorly and ill-nourished, as indeed do most of the infants I've seen here. The village children, in particular, seem universally dirty and predisposed to disease. I am told that they are often unwanted, and therefore neglected, and the number of children in local institutions is said to be formidable. All the time one is up against the financial problem: the patients have already paid the hospital for the consultation; can they also afford to pay for an X-ray, a blood-test, the necessary drugs, even a second visit?

5 December. Feeling awful with some sort of prolonged 'flu, sore throat, headache and diarrhoea, so that I can't feel confident in attending any social occasion and last night, having dragged myself to a splendid concert by the visiting Graz Chamber Orchestra, had to leave abruptly in the middle of Mozart's Salzburg Symphony to spend a dreary half-hour in the basement, squatting in an Iranian lavatory. Of course, no toilet-paper.

On top of all this, the dread of impending ructions when I get home on Christmas Eve: a scene with my hospital colleagues who maintain that I have been unfair to my *locum tenens,* a charming and very competent Indian lady, by returning unexpectedly early and so depriving her of a month's salary and employment; and recriminations from my wife, who feels that I have let the side down and seems – from here – to prefer a husband in exile who can be sent Christmas presents and parcels to one actually on the spot.

However, I have finished *Lytton Strachey,* every one of its 1,144 pages, and am very glad to have read it. I do not consider it as a biography of the first class; for that, the author must evidence some identification with his subject and this is not very apparent here. And indeed, to my mind, the most *felt* character in the work is that of Carrington, who loved Strachey so deeply as to kill herself a few weeks after his death. There's really no need now for anyone to write *her* life; it's all here. I am amazed, medically speaking, at the total inability of several really eminent clinicians, in 1932, to diagnose Strachey's stomach cancer; one cannot believe that this would have been the case today – though the outcome would still have been the same. I was grateful to have been reminded of the moving poem Tichborne wrote in the Tower while awaiting execution for conspiracy against Queen Elizabeth, the wonderful line:

And now I die, and now I was but made

There is nothing like this, the looking at your Death over your left shoulder as Carlos Castaneda tells us, to put problems of daily life in their proper perspective. However, it's irritating to reflect that my life would go more smoothly if only I had more *nous*. The fact is that I do not know what I want; though I do know what I *don't* want. And I am suddenly struck with the awful thought that perhaps most men go through life with this same unspecified and unsatisfied yearning, in a state of quiet despair. Happiness always seems to come fortuitously, obliquely, to be associated with long walks with friends, conversation, drinking in the sun (in both senses). I cannot – at the moment – recall a single occasion when some planned happy event was fully realized; but there have been many occasions when happiness came as a unexpected surprise, a by-product, a bonus. I have a very expensive hi-fi outfit but rarely use it because I know exactly what I shall hear and how it will sound; but to switch on the radio and catch by chance some well-loved music is the most delicious surprise. It is a datum, not a captum. This would seem to be related to the theme of responsibility and planning and being grown-up and a parent. I don't like planning; the most you can hope for is that things will turn out as you intended them to – but who are you to decide? I prefer unexpected surprises, goodies given by some anonymous parent; and as the conditions for such serendipity are steadily deteriorating, the outlook is bleak. But there is always the possibility. Doris Lessing talks about the importance of really *seeing*, as a child sees, as an animal sees, and hence of having and possessing a scene or a situa-in itself and for itself. I know exactly what she means; but, unlike her, I cannot will it. In the late summer, one day's end at our Sussex home, I went out with the children to watch for the transit of some satellite. As we gazed over the folds and contours of that incomparable landscape, it grew dark. The darkness fell from the air, it sprang up from the purple earth, it grew and spread and blurred all outlines. Colours died and disappeared. I don't remember ever having watched this process before, yet it is one of the most magical and important a man can witness, and *this* I possess, now and always. One supposes that, after childhood, painters are some of the few who really *see* their subjects. Many writers – Castaneda, and the author of that splendid book *Games People Play,* as well as a host of others insist on the importance of *seeing.* But you cannot see things as they are without the eyes of a child, and though we all have a child within us, he may be very deeply buried. Perhaps the next best thing is to see through the eyes of one's own children, before the blindfolds have been put on; hence the advantages for me, in late middle life, in having twins of three.

7 December. A null day. Or almost. The first such for many years. I had to have the grippe – a vile malaise, prevalent here – to justify it, and tracheitis. But I do go to see my little curly-haired girl, now at home, and begin to feel a cautious optimism, or at least a lesser degree of pessimism. If not flourishing, she is obstinately not dying but holding her own, and smiling. She looks for all the world a convalescent. The malignant mass under her back muscles is no longer palpable. Of course, she is having radiotherapy, chemotherapy, the lot; and I recall that some of these tumours have been known to yield to treatment, or even to regress spontaneously, and the possibility of her being brought to see me in England in the spring is no longer so remote. Children with malignant disease do sometimes have the most unexpected and improbable of remissions; of recoveries it is perhaps best not to speak. Her mother, seeing that I am afflicted, presents me with a bag of sweet lemons – unknown at home – and of pyramidal tangerines from Bandar Abbas, a name which reminds me of Dorset and *Beau Geste.*

The rest of the day I spend sitting reading or sleeping at the hotel, a divine luxury for which I feel no trace of guilt; with this chest I should be in bed. The book is Meredith's *Evan Harrington,* which I have stolen from the Savage Club. Meredith's clear view of life, his splendid style, the tragedy of his own personal life, all endear him to me. Every now and then I have the urge to stop and copy out some phrase into my commonplace book – if I had one. One is constantly reminded of Peacock, whose son-in-law he was. I reflect on the matter of style. We can all recognize it and deduce an author from a specimen passage. And linguistic analysis is said to show that grammatical construction, sentence length and punctuation, are as specific to the writer as his fingerprints. So it is true, after all, that *le style, c'est l'homme même.* And then, why do we read at all? It is to see a view of life, one

hat is not ours and that may therefore illuminate by a sort of mental
riangulation our own problems; also, as Richard Hughes has said,
:o enjoy the process of identification. But I do so much, and increas-
ngly, agree with whoever it was who said that whenever a new book
:ame out, he reread an old one!

8 December. Before sunrise the mountains opposite seem like lead.
To the Saadi Hospital to operate, feeling like death with this damned
chest infection. All goes well until the very last stage, when an essential
instrument is missing. However, we manage, as one always can. Spend
two hours in the Medical School Library translating Colette. Then
some confused medical politics, in which I have to steer carefully to
avoid being called in to justify one or other side. Then back to the
hotel for a beer and sandwich in the bar and back to Meredith in my
room until my eyes close in the hot afternoon sunshine. If it weren't
all so artificial and out of time, this would be a splendid way to live.
How best to live? As if one had the choice!

9 December. Am called away for a consultation at the local hospital
for joint-diseases. There is a lot of this here – but rheumatoid, not
osteoarthritis. Then a ward-round, the young internes submitting un-
questioningly to the pontifications of their teachers, as if they were
oracles. But one of them *does* question; and him I mark down for a
tour in England.

10 December. Ispahan. In the plane on the way there, I am unclear
whether I am merely being taken for the ride by a group of colleagues
going to Ispahan to conduct examinations, or am really expected to
take part. Probably both. When we arrive the temperature is, for the
first time here in my experience, well below zero. Ispahan has a more
brutal style and character than Shiraz, the people are more purposive
and work harder; there is heavy industry, a large steel works run by
the Russians. We are not, to my disappointment, staying at the legend-
ary Shah Abbas. Nevertheless, our hotel has a floor-show with some
marvellous singing. It is difficult to believe we are in the heart of a
stony wilderness.

11 December. I find I do have to sing for my bread and butter. Am
carried off to the examining board at the Medical School. We all

sit down round a long boardroom table to construct examination questions which, in my case, have to be translated into Farsi, all done with much good-natured banter and many tiny cups of delicious tea; and it is only later that I realize that one reason why all this has been left to the very last moment, to the very day of the examination, is that it prevents any chance of leakage. The examination is to decide whether certain of the younger doctors are fit to be classed as specialists or selected for specialist training, and we are here as outside assessors. I am either doing very well to be here, or am being promoted (Parkinson) to my own level of inefficiency.

Items of news are proffered during lulls for conversation. The University of Teheran is closed by a students' strike; no word of this has been allowed to appear in the newspapers. Renal dialysis in Teheran costs 150,000 - 200,000 toumans a year for private patients – some £10,000 - 14,000; so for ordinary patients, it is virtually non-existent. Understandably, renal transplantation is not making much headway here!

My part done, I have to sit for another two hours in a state of acute boredom while my colleagues continue with their general surgical questions in unintelligible Farsi. Am able to endure this largely owing to early training in sitting through synagogue services in Hebrew. The older I get, the more I am convinced, with Freud, that the first thing is to endure life; or is that a manifestation of depression, his and mine? There is a very wide spectrum between joy and endurance, and we have all to travel from one end to the other; the trouble is that joy insists on raising its head at rare and unexpected moments, and this makes us think that if we could only discover, and reproduce, the appropriate conditions, we could make her a more permanent guest. But not all our contriving will do so; and so we are never satisfied. I think of Colette's remark to a young man who complained of being unhappy: 'What on earth makes you think you should be happy? Work!'

On the subject of happiness, there is something that is no less a blessing, and that is relief from pain.

I remember a period of intense personal unhappiness when I was also engaged in a piece of research which required, from time to time, a detailed application to the microscope for long stretches. Each time I raised my head from the eyepiece after a session, there was a moment

– transient but very real – when I realized that I had not been experiencing the pain for a period and that it had not yet begun again. In this pause lay happiness. And I recall Camus's essay on the *Myth of Sisyphus,* doomed endlessly to toil at pushing his rock uphill and yet in possession of a moment, when he had done this and before it was all to do again, when he might be called happy. Or like a time when I burnt my hand so severely that only holding it under the cold tap gave relief – it was better than morphia – and yet one could not do this for ever. So that there was a moment, after removing one's hand from the flow, when the pain had been absent and would soon inevitably recommence, but had not yet done so. This was the most excruciating physical suffering I have ever experienced; and yet I cannot recreate it in memory or imagination. The burn was occasioned by using potassium chlorate in the garden, wearing gloves. Unless these are rubber they become impregnated, so that when you later make a bonfire the glove flares up and is pulled off with an underlying glove of burnt skin. I was afraid then that I might never be able to operate again, that my surgical career was finished. But my local doctor, whom we all love and trust implicitly, proved otherwise and I made a complete recovery. And all this happened at a time when I was convalescing from a coronary episode! Perhaps I should say a word about this.

Like most doctors, I have always had a peculiar fear and horror of succumbing to coronary thrombosis, the doctors' disease; and have computed too often the contributing factors thereto – anxiety, smoking, a sedentary life, overweight – so common in the medical life. I have also suffered from pseudo-coronary hysterical symptoms on occasion, as we all do. But some years ago I spent a whole day in the theatre; and began the next day, already exhausted, on a crowded and trying outpatient clinic, in the middle of which, as is my wont, I had to perform several manipulations under anaesthesia. The first of these was for a knee so stiff that all my force could not make it yield; and while so engaged I was seized with a most fundamental kind of spasm in the chest. It gave rise to the classical *angor animi,* but stopped when I stopped; so, foolishly, I went on to the next case, a spinal manipulation, for the patient was waiting. This time there was no doubt; the spasm returned, and brought me to the ground. I was taken and laid on a couch and lay there, not quite in terror, but with the mood, if not the words: *If it be Thy will, let this cup pass from me.* It did pass. I was filled with anti-coagulant drugs and carried off by ambulance to a medical bed at an adjacent hospital. I had had the experience of dying without actual death.

After I left hospital I experienced the resurgent enthusiasm for life which is typical in such circumstances, rather as Graham Greene describes after each round of his Russian roulette had proved a blank. But it did not last; it does not last; and it has left me with an undiminished terror of death. This gets worse as I get older; there are two things – at least – which distinguish man from the beasts: one is his capacity for continuous hard work, the other is the knowledge that he is going to die. And at my present age, at certain times, particularly birthdays, I feel like an animal being dragged to the slaughterhouse and already aware of the smell of blood.

It is bitterly cold in Ispahan this evening, the cold of a North European winter. We visit the Maidan at sunset. This combination of space and architecture where the Court used to watch polo, the great rectangle, with its two enormous coloured domes, constitutes a singularly elegant whole. It illustrates the felicitous and satisfying effect of proportion on the human spirit, which tends to become mean or elevated according to what is presented to it architecturally. No one can fail to be ennobled by contemplating the High Street at Thame, while the Old Kent Road never fails to be demeaning.

There are also the bazaar, the enamellers, the engravers, the carpet-makers, and many other fascinating sights. But I am still thinking of the subject of work as a defence against the universe, that it is essential, an occupational therapy for the disease of life, (though there are other mechanisms, such as the book-bed-bath defence system described by Cyril Connolly in that wonderful book, *The Unquiet Grave*). And yet Freud points out, in his so humane and soberingly pessimistic work, *Civilisation and its Discontents*, that although work is a sovereign remedy for most of man's ills, it is not one to which he willingly submits, and that, left to himself, he would prefer to be idle. For work, as for eating, appetite comes in the execution. Yet work brings other ills, those of monotony and repetition, and how are we to deal with these? A Christian may say that it has to be liturgicized, consecrated to the glory of God. Kierkegaard has a passage about the knight of repetition who transfigures the life of everyday.

The only remedy I know is that of frequent change, not to allow anything to last too long; but how to apply this to marriage or parent-hood? Perhaps marriage would benefit by the institution of sabbatical leave – a period of no questions asked from which one would return invigorated, ready to apply to an old relationship the lessons learned in some foreign field.

12 December. As I do not keep a commonplace book, let me insert here a comment from George Eliot:

'There is no private life which has not been determined by a wider public life.' How true, how pregnant.

13 December. Back in Shiraz. The nine o'clock Nemazee lecture for all comers. This morning a brilliant young Boston professor, talking about an extremely rare blood disorder in an intense American evangelistic style. It is dazzling, and meant to dazzle; and it reminds me of the existence of the big-time international medical circuit, which many world-famous authorities spend a great part of the year travelling. But is this what Iran wants, or needs now? The medical situation here sometimes seems like a pyramid standing on its apex - high-powered abstruse discussions tapering down to indifferent general practitioner services, local neglect and poverty; I have found no evidence of the existence of any useful liaison between the hospital service and the local doctors. Most patients who turn up at the out-patients clinics seem to do so on their own initiative. True, there must exist – and be seen to exist – some centres of excellence, some workers at the growing-points of medical science, but. . . . As it is, the hospitals are like casualty clearing stations dealing with a flood of victims of disease and injury which, though never abolished, could be reduced to a trickle by increasing the standards of general nutrition and hygiene. But the same applies, *pari passu*, as the medical scene moves west. What have we to boast of in the UK, a country which allows six hundred men in their prime to die needlessly every week because it cannot or will not do away with smoking?

17 December. Three days to lift-off. Spirits rise. The usual nonsense: waiting about in offices, making innumerable telephone calls to administrators before I can collect my salary.

Operating today, find myself increasingly irritable. The proper instruments are not available, it is impossible to communicate, I find myself shouting. In the middle of all this I raise my eyes to see surely the most splendid view from any operating theatre, the vast window filled with the expanse of mountains to the north, very close, drenched in sunlight.

Worse this afternoon – two hours to see three patients; no notes, no X-rays, no interpreter. I endeavour to accept the situation by imagining how I would feel if one of the Indian doctors working in my own hospital at home were to curse the natives for not speaking Urdu, or complained of not having an interpeter at hand. But it does not help; after all, I am the VIP out of the sky. And that thought jostles an elusive memory, a memory of a situation in which a man, aware of his own superior gifts, is increasingly irritated because those about him fail to recognize this superiority, frustrate him, treat him as deranged, in need of radical treatment. I cannot track this down. It is not Gulliver in Lilliput, though on those lines. It comes through after walking the length of the Zand: H. G. Wells's *The Country of the Blind*. That its protagonist could see, was the only one to see, stood him in no stead at all. Chastening.

How difficult it is to quarrel with anyone by letter, let alone one's wife, when there is a time-lapse of five to ten days in the correspondence. I write in an irritable mood, cool down after forty-eight hours and despatch a more peaceful missive, expect a reply in like tone and am shattered by the riposte to the original letter – at which moment, no doubt, she is wishing she had been softer. Quarrelling by post takes considerable animus and obstinacy, but is by no means unrewarding. I've only once so much regretted a virulent effusion that I asked our village postmaster to let me have it back; and that was difficult, for by that time it had ceased to be my property. But he consented when I went into a little detail! I've nothing against invective, from or against me, but it should be honest and whole-hearted and then end in laughter. Venom is another matter, and I can neither bear to be sarcastic nor to have sarcasm used against me.

The last few days go in a rush. The feeling of impending change, or loss, makes life more vivid; if only we could always realize that we die tomorrow. I came here primarily to escape from the acceleration of time that afflicts us all after the age of forty, though I recall first experiencing this is my teens. After fifty one begins to feel like a space-traveller, the galaxies receding at an ever-increasing speed.

There are ways of dealing with this, the shock tactics of a violent change of scene, a love affair, identification with a child; and coming here was one of these.

A serio-comic last day. I never gave my carefully rehearsed lecture on hip-replacement after all. Time did not allow. A farewell lunch in my honour at the University Club, Vice-Dean and all. Presumably the Dean would have been there had he not been away with a delegation to study acupuncture in China. In the morning I had picked up my hotel bill – never again shall I be faced with one for several hundred pounds; but it is less than it might have been, thanks to the kindness and generosity of the owner. My colleagues tell me that it is customary for the University to pick up the tab; but when I try this out half-heartedly, there is nothing doing.

I think of the private patients I have operated on; so far I have received no fees, nor do I expect to. I am not sufficiently ruthless, explanations are too difficult, and when, that night, I call to say good-bye to my little curly-haired girl, she presents me with a most beautiful and intricately-worked box; that takes the place of the whacking fee I might reasonably have expected. So, ruefully, I leave Shiraz about a thousand pounds poorer than I need have done, and because of an inherent inability to demand or haggle over money which is perhaps an over-reaction to the importance my parents always accorded this in business life.

And that is not all. By dint of repeated application and waiting about in corridors, I had managed to secure my salary in banknotes or enormous numbers of rials – a sum of about £1,000, half of which was required for hotel bills and air-fare. So the remainder represented my rather meagre earnings for the whole of my stay. Shortly before the banks close I take this moiety to the Saderat Bank and naïvely – as I now see – ask for it to be changed into English currency. I have decided not to have it credited to my Guernsey account after all and have an infantile desire to present my wife with a wad of £20 notes. But it is not to be be, £50 is the limit. Well, then, can I not change it in England? Again, no; the rial is worthless in the UK. It is too late to make the detailed arrangements for a transfer. My heart sinks. I feel trapped in a Catch 22 situation, like those authors who earn a million roubles in royalties which they are not allowed to take out of the Soviet Union. I have wild thoughts of buying a diamond or two to smuggle through. I am bitter against the University, which had assured me in writing that money earned could be taken out of the country.

However, at a farewell session at the Hospital I complain to my colleagues and one of them knows a bank-manager, to whom we repair. Over lime-juice and soda all is settled. Travellers' cheques can be bought. A messenger is sent out to the bazaar with my 5,000 rial notes, and returns with £20 notes bought at a ruinous rate of exchange. I lose £50 on the deal; but by this time I am determined to fly out the next day with all the cash I can lay my hands on rather than await the doubtful intricacies of credit transfer. Of course, as this is Iran, there has to be a *quid pro quo*. The manager has a son at school in England. Can I find him an English home for the holidays, my own perhaps? I say I will. A last-night restaurant entertainment.

I have, during this rush, been disturbed by a telegram from my wife asking whether my flight-plan still stands as there is no confirmation at home, and stating: 'Julian in Home Office explosion.' Julian is my son, who is a civil servant. I have read of the explosion a day or two before. But what does 'in Home Office explosion' mean? It seems designed to alarm rather than inform, a peculiar item of information presumably meant to indicate that he is not actually dead. (Only after my return home do I discover that the Iranian post office had omitted to include the despatched word 'uninjured'!) All this makes me feel that it would be wise to visit the airline office to check my flight. Oh yes, Teheran to London is OK, but the first leg, Shiraz–Teheran tomorrow, has been postponed for two hours. I fume. I could have given my lecture after all. And if I had not happened to drop in, how would I have been expected to know? Oh, all would have been well, they had left a message at the hotel. (They had not.)

The next day, Dr K., radiologist to the Hospital, uncle of my curly-haired girl and also somehow related to the hotel manager – which is how the whole of Shiraz knows about the child and her operation – drives me to the airport. I am moved to be leaving this place with its splendid climate, where I have received nothing but courtesy and respect, and where I have lived satisfactorily a solitary life. Waiting in the departure lounge, there is a bustle outside. A car disgorges a man on crutches, his leg in plaster, supported by three friends one waving a bundle of papers and X-rays. A, literally, last-minute consultation takes place under the interested gaze of a number of pass engers, no doubt distracting them from fears of air travel. Dr K. looks on embarrassed, as well he may, since it is pretty obvious that he has set up the whole thing. Once again I am too anxious to be allowed to make my getaway to demand my rightful fee. But at last we are airborne. Impressed, as always, with Iran Air's internal services, which are casual, efficient and comfortable – despite the fact that the previous week has seen a tremendous airlift of pilgrims to Mecca, paid for by the Government, all the pilgrims with identical suitcases bound with the national colours.

Again met in Teheran by my assistant's wife, plus his brother, a police captain – which makes progress notably easier – plus the daughter of my clinic nurse in London, who is working with the Iran National Ballet Company. Spend the rest of the day in various private houses, overfed, unable to communicate, and driven to solitary reading.

No sleep, as I have decided to try to catch an earlier flight, at 6.45. No joy, driving through the featureless plains of Teheran in the pre-dawn to find no seat available. Offered another flight, via Beirut, but refuse: Beirut is where the hijackers get on. So take my original 10 a.m. flight. Everyone uneasy, after the massacre at Rome Airport earlier this week. The security precautions are strict, except for heavy baggage, but child's play compared to what happens at Tel Aviv, where even transit passengers are searched rigorously. In between there has been a scenically magnificent flight the length of Turkey, then a dogleg down the Mediterranean off Syria and the Lebanon to avoid overflying 'sensitive' areas; we travel at least twice as far as necessary. There is still an uneasy and not unspoken feeling that a bomb may yet explode in the luggage-hold between Tel Aviv and London. Not only does one, in flying, have to barter safety for speed – if playgoing requires a temporary suspension of disbelief, flying demands a temporary disbelief in suspension – but one has to calculate, from sketchy data, which times and routes are less likely to see one blown to pieces or landing unexpectedly somewhere on the Persian Gulf.

But we are at Heathrow – dark, cold and wet at four in the afternoon. Met, to my joy, by my family – the joy including not having to face a single-handed journey with heavy luggage to Victoria, across London to Charing Cross, and then down to Sussex. Furious bad-mannered Christmas Eve driving despite the petrol shortage. We are all worn out by the time we get home.

27 December. England, home. Today, two days after Christmas, satiated and with a good excuse, I drove thirty miles to the hospital. The woman I came to see, an elderly seventy-five, lay unable to move, needles dripping fluid into her veins, a catheter in her bladder, relatives grouped around. The previous night she had fallen and hurt her neck. There is no fracture or dislocation, but the spinal cord has been severely damaged. Both legs and the left arm are paralysed; there is no sensation below the collar-bones. This kind of case is rare; the prognosis is nil. She will develop pressure-sores and cystitis, and die miserably. I tell the relatives as much, in an edited version; sometimes it is best to give the bad news in its totality. I often search my motives strictly over this, but don't find any trace of enjoying my power as an arbiter of life and death. This is just the sort of case in which, in a few years time, the relatives may well have the right to raise the question of euthanasia. It would not be unreasonable, but I would not do it, and I am glad I shall be retired by then. As I have said, these cases are rare, but we did have a somewhat similar one last year and the patient recovered against all expectations. I am sure the present patient won't do so. (She did not, in fact, see the New Year in.) However, were we ever to start killing off our supposedly hopeless cases – ostensibly for *their* sake, but to a large extent for our own, that is the relatives, doctors, nurses, in other words the community – we would no longer try so hard to keep them alive. Let the euthanasiasts enlist their own corps of butchers; I want no part of it.

I remember this time last year – another woman, fortyish, operated on on Christmas Eve for a prolapsed disc. She was glowing and contented, had had a good operation and knew it. The pain that had never left her for a single day for six months had gone. She presented me with some cigars. But my true Christmas gift was to see her well and happy, and to have had the privilege of making her so. I owed her much more than she owed me; but as it was impossible to explain this, I brusquely waved away her thanks and told her to begin walking. Nevertheless, we were both well satisfied; it was a true symbiosis of surgeon and patient.

Disc operations vary greatly. They may take as little as fifteen minutes or a couple of hours. They may produce an immediate and lasting cure, or usher in a lifetime of recurrent disability and further operations. It is best if the first operation is the only one, for every subsequent interference provokes fibrosis around the nerve-roots. In this case, when the affected root was gently eased off the protrusion over which it was stretched, a plunge of the forceps brought away a sequestrated mass of disc material the size of a plover's egg. It was like catching a really sizeable fish at one's first cast.

As most of the patients have gone home for the holiday – an infallible resurrectionist! – I am able to get home early in a short but gloriously sunny afternoon, prune my roses and burn the prunings before dark. The house is glowing with post-festival relaxation and the grave games of children. It begins to seem possible to start all over again in the New Year.

*

End of January. I write this as a patient in a hospital room. To-morrow I am being operated on for varicose veins, my first operation, my first anaesthetic. I have just been shaved and feel like a plucked chicken; they say it's worse when the hairs start growing again. I have the usual presentiments of doctors about to undergo surgery, calculate the risks. But now I am in the grip of the machine, rapidly being reduced to an object on the conveyor-belt, a number tied to my wrist. I feel resigned; and this is as it should be.

I don't want to be anaesthetized – it's like putting one's head under water, which I've never been able to do. But the surgeon refuses to work under local anaesthesia, which is admittedly a great strain on both parties. (In the event, the premedication produces such a blissful state of euphoria, that I can well understand why certain people prefer drugs to real life.)

Perhaps I am unusual in not needing the oblivion of an anaesthetic. For, though a great coward, I am good at standing physical pain, never have an anaesthetic for dental treatment, broke my back a few months ago and was digging in the garden a few days later. Yet I am afraid of death and think of it every day of my life, casting an occasional glance over my left shoulder. There have been times when the fear of death has been so overwhelming that I have cried out aloud:

'God help me!' This happened on my last birthday, always a menacing and unsettling anniversary. Walking along a stretch of road in southern France, I saw my shadow stretched blue before me, vividly recalling Francis Bacon's great paintings of Van Gogh on the road to Arles. I *saw* my death coming towards me. In the agony of these moments – they do not come often – the human condition seems precisely as Pascal described it:

> Picture a number of men in chains, all condemned to death, some of whom are slaughtered daily in front of the others, while those who remain see their own condition in that of their fellows, and, regarding each other sorrowfully and without hope, await their own turn. That is the image of the human condition.

I recall, in adolescence, first encountering this terror and being amazed that grown-ups were capable of going on living with this knowledge. I have noticed that women do not fear death as much as men; but then, they are the creators of life. And Man, terrified by death, turns towards Woman, who put him into this world, in an attempt to get back where he came from. It is in this sense that Eve brought death into the world and in this sense that sex is an alternative to the fear of death. It is only incidental that copulation is enjoyable; and Man's sadness after coitus is the measure of his failure to return to his origins. Man and animals copulate; only men long for union. I think that Freud says somewhere that the fear of death is not natural, that it is founded on guilt, that we cannot in fact envisage our own death and that the unconscious considers itself immortal. But the trouble is that we envisage it only too well. The cure may be to realize that we do not, when it comes, see our death objectively from the outside, a matter for pathos, a lapsing into oblivion. We experience death from *within* life, an arrival at a terminus; we shall not still be around afterwards to feel sorry for ourselves.

The operation is over. The sun is shining. The dark thoughts about mortality and death have temporarily receded. I have been for a walk. My leg, minus its veins, aches abominably. Every surgeon should personally experience at least one operation, so long as it does not undermine his capacity to treat the patient on the table as a thing. On the second day, post-operative blues set in. This is so common as to be almost routine; even the smallest operation tends to unleash our latent depression. My surgeon confesses that, when *he* had an operation, he burst into tears on the second day.

A week later I still feel as if I have been knocked down and trampled on. I am reminded, in terms of my own body, that a surgical operation is only a special form of assault and battery, legally so if done without consent. Back at home, I can still only walk a mile. It amazes me now to think of how, after some colossal hip operation, I cajole and bully my patients to get out of bed and walk by the second or third day, and that most of them actually do this and don't seem too unhappy. Physical injury of any kind is degrading, humiliating, distressing and depressing. But the real trouble is that we do not expect to encounter it as our ancestors did, and no longer have the same inner resources to meet it with.

As I approach sixty, I feel more and more that many of the questions that had to be swept unanswered under the carpet at the end of adolescence, return now, as unanswerable as ever and more urgent. They relate to the nature of our fragile lives on this rind of a probably unique planet, sweeping in its compound motion through the desolate spaces of a universe that is utterly hostile, utterly non-human, utterly devoid of any moral order. I feel, wrapping up for the difficult passes ahead, that all we can do is to cling to one another in the dark; and that we have a contract with one another so simple and so important that we forget it most of the time: we must love one another or die; we must love one another *and* die; kindness is all.

Part Two

Looking Back

1

Lusisti satis, edisti satis,
atque bibisti;
Tempus abire tibi est.

HORACE

You have wined and dined and indulged enough; it is time to go.
Time, said Horace, because if you can't live aright, give way to those
who can, before the younger ones laugh at your self-indulgence, then
turn you out. But just before going, at around sixty, there is always
the temptation to a self-justifying autobiography or, at least, to the
apologia pro vita sua of an after-dinner speech. I have often wondered as to the precise significance to the protagonists of these per-
formances. Are they of the nature of a Roman triumph, with the
victor displaying his spoils? Is it, as Graham Greene observes in
another context, a matter of the prisoner serving a life sentence being
discharged on consideration of good behaviour, and with a small
pension? Or is it, perhaps, that every dog has its day? In any case, it
provides an opportunity not to be missed to say what one likes to
one's peers with little fear of reply or reprisal; with luck one will be
dead before the writs start to come in. It is a massive act of catharsis,
a purging of the pent-up loathings and longings of a lifetime, a final
act of self-justification before the mausoleum looms. And how
attractive, after so long behind the scenes, to have just a few moments
before the audience!

It may be that the attempt is bound to fail. After thirty years (for
which I am profoundly grateful) as a consultant orthopaedic surgeon,
a branch of the profession which I have never for a moment regretted
adopting, it might be wiser to emulate the Lord Chief Justice who
said, at a farewell dinner: 'I have come prepared with two speeches, a
short one and a long one. The short one is "Thank you", and the long
one is "Thank you very much".' In any case, some selection is essen-

79

tial if the right message is to be put across.

In my case, there is also something else. I want to say to the laity: you take surgery and surgeons for granted. You accord us a certain measure of respect or – too often – regard us as state functionaries, like postmasters. Some of you cast us as gods, though most of us know better than to accept that role. Vast numbers of you have benefited from our services. We have improved the quality of your lives, snatched you back when you had already begun to cross the Styx. Not a few others curse the day you ever met us; for we are only human, and we can botch and bungle and interfere unnecessarily as well as anyone. But what none of you knows is what it *feels like* to be a surgeon; what a surgeon's life is like. No one knows this, not even one's wife or a medical colleague, only a fellow-surgeon. And so, to some extent, I can speak both to and for my fellows.

I do not intend to proceed in chronological order. Rather, like my beloved Colette, I shall dart hither and thither in time, a diary with the dates disarranged. Perhaps a good place to begin is at the point where the drab chrysalis turns into a gorgeous butterfly, when the underpaid, increasingly hopeless surgical registrar who has been hanging about the railings of Paradise sees the gates finally opened and is admitted to the glory of being a consultant. At least, that is what it was like immediately after the end of the last war. Permanent appointments were being made, surgeons were returning from the Forces and competition was intense: there might be as many as fifty or sixty applicants for some of the more attractive posts. The situation was a poignant one and not, perhaps, to be encountered in any other profession or calling. At one moment one was a penniless outsider, at the next, monarch of all one surveyed. 'Your chief,' I was solemnly told by the house-surgeon when I began as a student in the wards, 'your chief is God.' Even now this is still true to a remarkable degree. But the situation has otherwise greatly changed. I am informed that there is currently a large number of fully trained senior surgical registrars who will not apply for consultant posts: first, because with overtime pay (for which consultants are not and never have been paid) they are earning a good deal more than a consultant at the bottom of the ladder, and second, because they are waiting to see which way the medico-political cat is going to jump before deciding whether to stay in this country or to emigrate while the going is good.

In 1946, two years before the coming of the National Health Service, I was already a consultant for the London County Council Hospitals. But that was unimportant, little more than paid charitable work, although it did have the advantage that one was paid by the hour. So when, as was often the case, I operated away until midnight at some County Council Hospital (they were all named after rather obscure Anglo-Saxon saints), it was with the comforting thought that each hour meant so many more guineas in my pocket. But now I was anxious for an unpaid post as Honorary Orthopaedic Surgeon at a voluntary hospital. It was this that would set the cachet on my career, justify my newly-acquired Harley Street consulting-room, bring in, eventually, the private practice that would make my bank manager beam instead of threaten.

One of the things one had to do was to call on every member of the consulting staff of each hospital. And as one was firing into the brown, applying at perhaps a dozen metropolitan hospitals – as well as many in the provinces, each with a visiting staff of thirty or forty – this meant many a weary and footsore hour trudging the pavements of Harley Street and Wimpole Street to keep appointments which were often mere formalities but which, if omitted, might bring disaster at the appointment committee. 'Not a bad chap . . . but he didn't bother to call on me,' – a thumbs-down I was often to hear in later years from a colleague when I had finally arrived and was myself sitting at the right end of the boardroom table.

I had already envisaged the sort of job I wanted as early as 1944, when I left the army. It would be at the hospital of a county town hospital and would enable me to live in the country, in delectable surroundings yet only a short distance from the centre. I would be not *an* orthopaedic surgeon but *the* orthopaedic surgeon, a big fish in a not-so-small pool. I would meet the local architect, the local solicitor or the local accountant in the snug of the best hotel for a drink before lunch or at the end of the day, any day in the week. There would be a large and comfortable middle-class element in the population and the practice would be lucrative. There would be good walking and plenty of fresh air and sun.

But it was not to be. If one was to attain the coveted status, one had to try for everything that was offered and to accept the first offer. In my case it turned out to be a small hospital, delightful enough in itself, set on top of a hill in the middle of sprawling South London suburbia which was neither fish nor fowl, neither real town nor real country.

True, in those days one could drive from the suburbs to one's office in Harley Street or to one's club in a quarter of an hour, and park the car where one wished for as long as one wished. This was before the days of dense traffic and yellow lines. Now the logistics have changed and it has become a cruel penance, after a heavy day at the hospital, to drive hard against the traffic for the best part of an hour in order to attend some learned lecture at the Royal Society of Medicine, or to reach one's consulting-room and wearily slog home again. After years of this killing routine I have now retreated to rural Sussex, thirty miles from the hospital, and it takes me no longer to get there than it would a colleague living in Hampstead or Wimpole Street.

In any case, I had arrived! And I shall never forget the joys of being an honorary in those halcyon few years before the descent of the Health Service. One really was monarch of all one surveyed. One's name went up in gilt letters on the board in the front hall bearing the names of the members of the consultant staff. One was saluted by the porters, eyed quizzically by the older sisters and with more of a gleam by the younger ones. One sat on the Medical Committee and decided affairs of state. To this committee was summoned the hospital secretary (the entire administrative staff consisted of one man and a few girls where it has now pullulated into many score) who would click his heels and say 'Yes sir' and 'No sir', not having yet acquired the swagger and patronizing air he would adopt after the 'appointed day' of Aneurin Bevan in 1948. We could, in theory and almost in fact, do exactly what we liked, professionally speaking. There was no one to check our standards of performance (nor is there now). One was a Fellow of the Royal College of Surgeons and this implied the attainment of certain standards when applying for the job. But after appointment, one's conscience was the only guide. The patients certainly couldn't tell whether you were any good or not. If your mortality for a particular operation rose to more than was decent, the Chairman of the lay committee might ask, with the appropriate degree of embarrassment and circumlocution, exactly what was going on. The only possible judges of your excellence, or lack of it, would be your colleagues. But it is a fact of life that, because outpatient and operating sessions have to be dovetailed within a tight timetable, your colleagues are precisely those who will never be there to see you operate or conduct a clinic. You will occasionally run against them at lunch, and there the only skill that is apparent is conversational.

I soon learned to appreciate the truth of a remark made to me by one of the general surgeons who appointed me: 'Once you're on the staff of a London hospital, you're on your own!' I have already remarked that there is no need to go to the colonies to gain surgical experience; the material is all there in the outer suburbs – hundreds of thousands of potential patients, waiting to be plunged into. (That is why the great London teaching hospitals – Charing Cross, St George's – have had to move out there). And one is soon so busy, so much on the run – for one collects hospitals as a lepidopterist collects specimens and I was soon on the staff of no less than eleven hospitals south of the river – that it is only too easy to find oneself passing day after day, month after month, without ever speaking to a colleague in one's own discipline in an adjacent hospital group, or going to a scientific meeting. It is rather like being posted to Iceland or some other outpost during the war. Whether you maintain your civilized standards – in this case your surgical standards – depends entirely on yourself. You have got, somehow, to find time to read your specialist journal (and you will soon learn that, if you don't read a journal immediately it arrives, you never will), to attend the meetings of your specialist section at the Royal Society of Medicine, to get away once or twice a year for the gatherings of your national specialist association, to attend the regional orthopaedic club based on your area of London and the adjacent counties. This is important, if only to keep the spirit of emulation and keenness alive. For if you go to such meetings you will want to win the approval of your peers, to discuss difficult cases, to show your own successes and – to gain real popularity – your own failures. It took me some years to discover that showing how clever I was gained no friends or admirers at all. But when I began to show my mistakes – and mistakes are what one really learns from in surgery, though preferably those of others – then I began to win friends and influence people. To be superhuman may be impressive, but it is being human that's difficult.

Soon, too soon, you find that it is no longer possible to understand the articles printed in the *Lancet* or the *British Medical Journal* on any topics other than your own speciality. It is no good carrying a journal about under your arm in the hope that its contents will be assimilated by axillary absorption. This professional isolation particularly affects the more esoteric disciplines such as orthopaedic or opthalmic surgery since there is often only one exponent of each at any particular hospital, while there will always be more than one general surgeon. But there are ways round this. One is to find time to visit the clinics of those surgeons you most admire, and whose methods you want to study and perhaps adopt, in Europe and America; and this is best done by joining a surgical travelling club which goes abroad once or twice a year and may, perhaps, entertain some eminent visitors on its home ground from time to time. I gradually forged links with opposite numbers in Scandinavia and Western Europe which have lasted through the years.

One local problem arose from the fact that the general surgeons at my main hospital seemed to have decided to create an orthopaedic post merely to complete their range of advertised services. I really believe that they expected me to do little more than prescribe an occasional arch-support or artificial limb, and that the idea that I would compete with them for beds and operating time had never entered their heads. In fact such competition developed into a ferocious running battle that was never entirely resolved. From time to time there would be an armistice and boundary lines would be drawn in the wards, but this never lasted for long; some of my best friends are general surgeons, but when it comes to this kind of negotiation they are lying, treacherous bastards. They were only too glad to hand over the fracture clinics, which they had found a boring necessity; but for years I had to conduct my orthopaedic outpatient clinic in the boardroom. They could not prevent the admission of accident cases under my care; but they could and did slow down the admission of 'cold' orthopaedic cases for operation to a point where I could only work efficiently by discharging my patients so soon that we rapidly gained and held the national record for the shortest stay in hopsital after major surgical procedures.

But let me confess that I now feel rather like a space traveller whose home planet has been destroyed during his voyaging, so that he can never return. The hospital to which I was first appointed in 1946, and which I had to leave for a much bigger neighbouring institution a few years ago, has always held first place in my heart. In its time it was the neatest, busiest, prettiest, most efficient and *happiest* of little surgical hospitals. It has now been transformed into an institution largely devoted to preventing old persons from leaving this world and young ones from entering it. That is to say, half the beds are now geriatric and the other half gynaecological – and the latter are increasingly occupied by young women having 'social' abortions. If this is progress, I am glad I shall soon be retiring. All that is required to complete the job is a euthanasia department in the basement; and that will soon come if our trendy, progressive, left-wing, middle-class traitors have their way, for we – the doctors – have already sold the pass on abortion, which is murder. And if, as doctors, our left hands are increasingly occupied with the denial and destruction of life, it will take a remarkable feat of schizophrenia to prevent this from diluting and damaging the more traditional healing activities we carry on with our right hands.

*

The impact of the National Health Service on the medical profession in 1948 was a stunning one. I was in favour of it at the time, when it was an extremely unpopular attitude for one in the profession, as I was then a young socialist (I have since seen the light) and actually wrote a book about it for the layman. This I produced by taking down from Hansard everything that was said in the House during the passage of the Bill, dividing it into two piles – for and against – and throwing the latter away. I have to be honest and report that I now feel, thirty years later, that I threw away the wrong pile.

The immediate result in hospital life was the establishment of two kinds of committee: the mainly lay Hospital Management Committee and the Advisory Medical Committee of consultants. The former was a statutory body, the latter not, an initial cause for a sense of inferiority.

But let us deal with the medical body first. We did not know where the new set-up was going to lead. We did know that, from having been largely independent contractors, we were now exposed to domination by the Management Committee close at hand and, more remotely, by our new employers, the Regional Hospital Board. What we had already seen of our new masters did not inspire much confidence, for the new hospital administration had inherited the old untrained hacks from the old dispensation and the newer breed had yet to arrive. But administration was quite obviously pullulating, and its appetite grew by what it fed on.

Our medical committee, therefore, was uneasy. It was the kind of body where you had to know a man very well before you could call him by his surname, and which it was wiser to attend – if I may employ an Irishism – in case you were stabbed in the back when you weren't there. For, in the fear of the unknown, one's colleagues were torn between the laudable desire to stand united in the defence of professional standards and privileges, and the less laudable desire to curry favour with the new powers and carve out a small empire for their own specialities at whatever cost. The haggling over beds and boundaries and duties that was never to cease during the coming decades had begun. Meetings were always bewildered and bewildering, sometimes stormy, as new directives from above were studied and interpreted. Members would walk out, slamming the door behind them. I did so on one occasion. I recalled how, in adolescence, I had imagined those who exercised power on important committees as godlike disinterested figures, majestically dispensing right. Now I was a member of just such a committee, and I realized sharply that it was governed by the passions of the nursery. I suppose that the prevailing characteristic we shared was that of frank paranoia; and if ever I write a novel about the health service, that will be the name of the hero.

Here I should like to say a few words on the subject of hospital administration in general. I must confess, at the outset, to being hopelessly biased. I regard administration as, at best, a necessary evil – no less evil for being necessary – and administrators as Whitmans's 'crawling serpentine men, the born freedom sellers of the earth'. I loathe and detest administration and administrators, with their 'duplicate grey standard faces', perhaps not entirely with reason, but with sufficient reason. I work, preferably and rather secretively, on my own. I want a room in which to see my patients, proper equipment (in fact very little) to deal with them, and then to be left alone. I don't like being interfered with, or having to haggle – first with a score of colleagues and then with unseen, stony-faced officials – for my share of a limited supply of money, space and services. For this means that it is not enough to be a good clinician; you have to be a politician as well. And the more time and energy you spend on putting your own case in committee, the more such power will come to be an end in itself, and the less initiative will be left to treat your patients.

Let me say at once that I am opposed to medical men serving on predominantly lay committees at almost any level. The laymen like to have one or two doctors there so that they may say they have 'consulted' the medical interest; but we have learnt the hard way just how genuine such consultation is. When an administrator proposes 'a free and frank discussion', it is time to stand with your back to the wall. At best, the doctor is an uneasy hostage of the committee, knowing that he cannot possibly fairly represent or defend his colleagues' multiple interests there. At worst, he goes over to the other side, identifies with the lay source of power, and uses his opportunities to expand his power base in his own department. It is to be noted that the doctors who serve on such committees are rarely those most devoted to clinical work; these are too busy in the wards or the operating theatres. No, it is the pathologists and other fringe workers who tend to fill these posts. It seems to me that our duty, as doctors, is to formulate and clearly express to the laymen what we need to treat our patients efficiently, and so to place the responsibility for any shortcomings squarely where it belongs.

I have not sat on a committee of any kind for at least ten years, and without any loss. My work has been unaffected and my blood-pressure lower. The latest development is an attempt to make the doctors identify themselves more closely with administration by forming what are vacuously known as 'cog-wheel' committees, each dealing with a particular discipline, say surgery or gynaecology, and all intermeshing and liaising (horrid word!) with lay authority. It is as if the Madam of a brothel had succeeded in persuading the inmates not only to pursue their regular duties but to keep the books as well!

For the hospital consultant, administration has always tended to be peripheral to his field of work. True, after 1948, there was the local management committee, but his actual employers were the Regional Hospital Board, which governed the hospital services of millions of people over a large slice of England from palatial offices many miles away. One hardly ever saw these figures, save when they would pay a brief visit to promulgate some new policy or, more often – notably more often – to abandon an old one. And this remoteness was, and still is, demoralizing. It is not amusing for the staff of a hospital to learn, for the first time, from the newspapers that the institution to which they have devoted their lives is to be closed down, or to have its functions radically altered. It has happened in the past. It happens still, for they never learn. Again, I do not recall that, at any time during my thirty years, an administrator ever came to ask me if I was happy in my work, if there was anything I needed, if there were any suggestions or complaints I cared to make. As I have said, the human being cannot pat himself on the back; the good Lord knows that we cannot dispense entirely with some form of recognition and encouragement. There are, of course, the provocative merit or distinction awards. But these are not worn openly and proudly as evidence of acknowledgment of good work, as one may wear the rosette of the Legion of Honour. On the contrary, they give rise to so much jealousy and manoeuvring that they are never talked about at all. No one dares mention that he has an award for fear of arousing hostility and envy in the less fortunate. It was a badly conceived system and I hope it soon perishes. It was always heavily loaded in favour of the teaching hospitals; and to us in the suburbs or provinces, with our far smaller private practices, the whole set-up seemed unfair. That is, until one received an award oneself, out of the blue. Then it was all right.

But to return to local hospital administration. As I have said, initially its members were largely untrained. I admit that all this may now have changed. I have no doubt that there exist staff colleges for career employees of the service, that there is an established profession of health service administrators with its own standards and proprieties. But I work at the coal-face; and I can only sadly record that, as administration has multiplied and prospered, the health service itself, what one can actually do for the patient, has disintegrated and decayed. More of this later.

I have to record, too, that there exists, latent or overt, a hostility between doctors and administrators that is by no means one-sided. Too many administrators simply do not like the doctors. They see them as independent contractors with their own standards of excellence, men and women of vocation; they envy and hate these standards and fear that they are themselves looked down upon. The result is that, just as a famous publisher is said to have once made the heartfelt remark that publishing would be a splendid business if one could only dispense with the authors, so our administrators too often give the impression that the health service would be very much better without the doctors. Especially the consultants, those moody and demanding *prima donnas* who have the supreme insolence of working for enormously extended hours with no additional payment, a form of gratuitous endeavour of which no self-respecting administrator who locked his office door at five would ever be guilty.

I may mention here that, on the days I operate, I am paid for a session of two and a half hours. But, like all my colleagues, I had never counted my hours of work, or not until Barabara Castle recently forced us to do so. I have habitually operated for four, six, or eight hours, sometimes all day from before dawn till after dusk in winter. This is partly because it is my nature to be obsessional about work, partly because there is always more work than can be done; but partly, I now admit, to tease the administrators, who cannot understand, and never will be able to understand, what it is that makes a man work twice or three times the hours he is paid for.

I do know too that, over the years, I have had the greatest difficulty in obtaining quite elementary and essential facilities from administrators whose automatic response to a cry for help echoed Groucho Marx's theme song: 'Whatever it is, I'm against it!' When one has to see anything from fifty to a hundred and fifty patients in a clinic which nominally lasts three hours but may drag on for four or five, it is a simple matter of working efficiency to have a secretary at one's side, who can take down the clinical findings and make the clerical arrangements. But whenever I attempted to secure such a secretary for my department, I was met with blank, ununderstanding refusal. Why, if I had a secretary, all my colleagues would want one! This from a lay administrator who had a whole harem of personal secretaries and could not himself function for a moment without one. It took two years of unremitting struggles, with eventual appeals to friends in the House of Lords, before I could obtain what is now – and only in some places – taken for granted.

Another, and maddening, deficiency in our administrative colleagues – and some of the worst of these were medical men – lay in the lack of provision they made for genuine joint consultation. A great deal of lip-service was paid to the importance of putting us in the picture and seeking our opinions on hospital planning, but it really amounted to nothing. I have had, with many of my colleagues, the experience of devoting many committee hours over the years – hours that could ill be spared from clinical duties or relaxation, to the planning of a new hospital facility. And when it was all done, our advice was disregarded and the administrators walked off like Frank Sinatra, singing 'I did it my way!' The ineptness, the sheer inefficiency and wastefulness of much planning has to be seen from the inside to be believed. A wrong initial decision is made about where to site a new hospital complex; that done, money is thrown away in hundreds of thousands of pounds year after year to exploit the initial error; and eventually, after years of loss and struggle and planning and hoping, one is blandly informed from headquarters that the entire project has been dropped. Decisions and directives change year by year until all is order, counter-order, confusion and chaos.

It is rather like that form of plant growth known as a cyme, where the leading point of the stem turns to one side, aborted, a side-shoot takes over, the process is repeated, and you end up with what seems like a straight stalk but is really the concealment of a number of failed intentions. We are familiar with this from the history of communist states. No matter how frequent the policy changes, the direct line of revolutionary progress must always be demonstrable. Nor must one ever commit the cardinal error of showing that the functionaries have erred, or of putting forward the common-sense solution that must be seen as coming only from them. That is an unforgivable solecism.

And the money thrown away because of these changed decisions, and from decisions implemented not on a basis of genuine need but from climbing on some popular medico-political bandwagon, such as the creation of expensive accident centres in places where they are not needed, because that is the currently fashionable thing to do! Hospitals, specialist units, are closed, developed, resited, switched to alternative use, staff are deployed and redeployed on no discernible plan or pattern whatever. I have often thought that, if one managed one's own affairs in such a fashion, one would soon be in the bankruptcy court. Alas, sometimes one does and is. But these people are supposed to be the *experts*. There is no limit to human stupidity against which, as Schiller says, the Gods themselves struggle in vain.

The worst of it all, and not only in the health service, is the prevailing delusion that the remedy for the deterioration in real resources and finances is an increase in the sophistication and expense of administration. Here is a local example, illustrated in a letter to *The Times* (February 1975) signed by several consultants. They write that the White Hart Hospital, Harrogate, which contained 170 beds for rheumatic patients and was closed in 1970 against medical advice on the grounds that it was structurally unsound and no money was available for repair, is now being converted into a conference and training centre for administrators, at a time when work on the Leeds General Infirmary and the Harrogate District Hospital has been stopped. So the number of beds available for such treatment in this national centre has been halved, and the waiting-list correspondingly lengthened, because of this arrogant distortion of priorities.

At a national level, the administration of the entire National Health Service was reorganized in 1974 with the intention of increasing the local integration and autonomy of hospitals, general practice and public health services. But the expected benefits have not materialized, the bureaucracy swells, and the whole endeavour is devouring funds that were meant for the patients. Thus, some hospital administrators have had their pay increased from £6,000 to £9,000 with no substantial increase in their work. A great deal of money has been spent in buying new offices and upgrading old ones. We still have the extraordinary spending spree at the end of the financial year.

To quantify: in the eight years, 1965-1973, total hospital administrative staff increased by 51 per cent. In the same period the number of beds occupied daily fell from 451,000 to 450,000. In 1965 there was one administrator or clerk to 9.5 occupied beds. In 1973 there was one to 5.6. Such is the NHS equivalent of inflation: too many staff chasing too few beds, the inverted pyramid with a small number of active workers at the apex and a mass of arse-in-air do-nothings at the base.

This splendid devolution is really an elaborate game of musical chairs that only masks the old hierarchical structure and is not accompanied by any real increase in local financial freedom and responsibility. The dead hand is still there. There is still close control by the Department of Health and Social Security. But there are more and more committees, more and more channels through which decisions must pass. And meanwhile, promotion of the administrators increasingly removes them from contact with hospital staffs of all grades. The Department, through its inept handling of the medical manpower situation, has savaged the hospital's capacity to be a training as well as a service facility. As ever, the reorganization plan was presented as a *fait accompli*, and no worthwhile modifications were permitted.

It is the same with nursing. The ill-starred Salmon Report, a few years ago, gave the highest financial rewards to those who deserted the wards for the ranks of senior administration. The outcome is that a ward sister, who used to be a woman of immense experience and ability, must now choose between abandoning her post to gain a higher salary and position in the sterility of an office-job – leaving the wards to be looked after by nice but sadly junior girls – or remain where her heart is in her work, but where she feels she is ordered about and looked down on. Here is the very essence of the evil – the fact that administration is hierarchical, when it ought to be no more than parallel with clinical responsibilities.

So, all in all, I have not much cause to like the administrators. They do not really understand us. They do not see, for instance, that men who work as hard as we do might benefit from the institution of sabbatical leave. I subscribe to all the old jokes about administrators: that there is an iron hand in the iron glove; that behind that ruthless inhuman exterior there beats a ruthless inhuman heart; that an administrator is a man who can enter a swing-door behind you and come out in front on the other side; that when an administrator has a glass eye, you can tell which one is false by its human expression. I equate administrators with Dante's 'evil counsellors', whose fate in hell was to be perpetually pursued by clouds of hornets. I often think of the old Scots story of the minister preaching the torments of hell to his congregation, of how the parched sinner would look up to God and beg a drop of water, how the Lord would remind him that he was in hell for his arrogance towards the meek in life, how the sinner would gasp: 'Lord! Lord! I didna ken, I didna ken!' and how the good Lord, in his justice and mercy, would look down and say: 'Well, ye ken the noo!' And I like to think that that sinner had been an administrator.

2

January 1975. Working to rule. Am torn between two quite opposed feelings: an unsuspected and unworthy elation at acting perversely – in refusing to see new patients or sign medical certificates or do routine operations (this lasts as few days as one's boyhood delight at release from school) – and a keen regret at not using to the full the talents I have, to meet what I feel to be my obligations. Attitudes doctors formerly regarded as unthinkable have become acceptable. It may well be that in a greedy, acquisitive society, which is what we have got, the strains imposed on the caring professions will become too great, that they will find themselves reduced to ordinary trade union activities. We have already seen this in the case of the nurses and the ancillary workers, and now we are seeing it in ourselves. It may be that duty and devotion have become the dirty words of the 1970s, in which case I should wish to resign from the human race, or at any rate from my profession.

So often in the past one has joined the middle-class chorus of criticism of trade unionists who put self-interest before the national interest. Is what we are doing now any better? Before trying to answer this I must note wrily the perverse pleasure of acting in a manner precisely contrary to one's usual obligations, calculated to destroy where one usually builds up; to wound the public instead of serve it; to inflict the maximum damage on the community, whether one is a miner, an electrician, an ambulance driver – or a doctor.

Morbid thoughts. Beneath our smooth conforming surfaces, how much hatred has been simmering against the formalized repression imposed by calling or trade. Now it is to be a holiday for the Id; the aggression it has cost us so much to repress can emerge, blinking, from its cave, uneasily flexing its new-found muscles. We long to hate – as a crowd. We need to hate – as a crowd. The ethos of the pack is entirely different from that of the individual. One man can only be a martyr; men can martyr others. A man is human; a crowd is sub-human. War – or the equivalent of war – is a biological and psychological necessity, and one of our major problems is that we badly need

93

a war and dare not have one. We all long to torture and kill, or see it done on our behalf, on the television. In 1984, if not before, we shall all want to stand with the crowds in Victory Square, watching the shuffling procession of prisoners of war.

But to return to working to rule. Like most such episodes, it is not entirely reasonable but none the less valid in terms of emotional commitment. The financial aspect, though important, is the least part. As so often happens in industrial disputes, a financial demand may be the only way of expressing a profound unhappiness about working conditions. As far as I am concerned, money is of little consequence as long as I am not actually without it. I tend to agree with Zola that money was invented to keep the tradesmen happy. Today, any rise in salary is immediately swallowed up in tax and consequential increases in prices; the money is literally rotten. I have always lived, like my old friend Montaigne in his time, from hand to mouth; the only question has been the size of the overdraft. And it is galling to know that the only financial problems of my opposite numbers – and many of my past pupils – in America, Canada, Australia, New Zealand, France and Germany is how to carry the money to the bank. I shall never know what it feels like to have money at my back. Although none of this worries me overmuch, it would be nice, as retirement looms, to be able to afford to work when and where I want to instead of being compelled to the same routine day after day, to work *gratuitously,* in the full sense of the word. There is also the question of one's status in society; a reasonable degree of respect would go a long way to compensate for an inadequate salary.

The root of the present problem is, I think, a form of paranoia, an uneasy feeling that one has been exploited too long. And one has. We all work far longer hours, unpaid, than is stipulated in our open-ended contracts. We are engaged for thirty hours or so a week and actually work anything up to 120! I must remain on call for emergencies for forty-four hours each week over and above my routine four-and-a-half-day contract. My operating lists continue for two or three times the scheduled period. The whole of the hospital side of the NHS was built up and has survived on the blood and bones of the obsessionally overworking part-time consultant. But he will never work like that again.

Yet none of us ever counted or thought of counting our hours until now, when an insensitive and obdurate Secretary of State, the Ugly

Duchess of the Cabinet, has succeeded in creating as much ill will in her negotiations with the consultants as she did not so long ago in an ill-advised attempt to discipline the unions. None of us would want to calculate our efforts if these were recompensed with appropriate status, independence and – yes – salary too. But our masters – or our mistress – want more than this. They want, ultimately, to make us full-time salaried servants of the state; whereas we see ourselves as independent contractors whose first duty is to our patients. They, the left wing of the Labour Party, want to eliminate private practice, first from the NHS (that is inevitable, though it does not justify the wholly illegal refusal of hospital ancillary workers to service private wards, an illegality notably condoned by the Government) and then, if they can, from the country altogether. It is exactly the same as in education: first introduce a national comprehensive service and then, and this is very important, eliminate or destroy every type of independent service – the public school, the private clinic – which might survive to provide unsettling standards, an ideal of excellence. People's memories are short and it is only a brief step to 1984, from 'You never had it so good!' to 'You never had anything else!' They cannot achieve their object now; we are not yet so cowed. But they will return to worry at it again and again, like jackals.

Yes, memories are short. We *did* once have a full-time salaried hospital medical service, that of the municipalities, such as the old London County Council. I am old enough to have known this and to have worked for it as a visiting consultant from the free world. And it was almost universally second-rate, its staff – with a few noteworthy exceptions – mediocre. For this kind of service attracts mediocrity, just as do municipal architectural and legal services; they are a haven for the less than excellent, the unadventurous and unenterprising. While it existed, hospital doctors were divided into two classes: those, in the voluntary sector, who struggled and aspired and set the standards, and those who had virtually sold out in return for a quiet life.

The precise danger of a full-time salaried service for hospital consultants is that it would reproduce the undesirable features of the old municipal services and, *at the same time,* abolish external standards of comparison in the zeal of the obsessional egalitarianism, the inverted élitism, of our present masters. It would become very difficult to create or maintain centres of excellence within such a system, and many young, and not so young, doctors would vote with their feet as they departed for other sectors of the English-speaking world – and for Europe, too, unless our left-wing 'internationalist' friends pull us out of the Community altogether. I am not saying that good work would be impossible within such a system, that good men could not function therein; that would be a monstrous over-assertion. But the scales would be weighted against them, for the spur to professional excellence is the freedom and independence which accompany the knowledge that success depends on one's own efforts.

Recently, a professional man came to me from an eastern European country for an operation which that country's medical services could not provide; he expressed the fervent hope that we should not reproduce here the situation in his own country where bureaucrats are all powerful and doctors dare not raise their heads. Our socialist friends may vehemently deny that these are their objectives; but this is what we shall get if they have their way. To be fair, I acknowledge that I have never experienced any administrative interference in my clinical work; but this is largely because of the existence of an independent private sector as a safeguard. When the surgeon is entirely a government servant, when there is no outside alternative employer or standard of reference, then the shadow of the state will fall across the consulting-room between him and his patient. Then the faceless administrators will be able to do what they have longed to do: to establish quotas and norms of working hours and patients seen per hour and operation times, all carefully costed, insidiously to lay down what patients should be given priority. When this type of quantification comes in at the door, excellence – which can never be quantified – will fly out of the window.

The Ugly Duchess denies that it is her intention to create, willy-nilly, a full-time salaried service, that those who wish to stay as they are can do so. But the new contracts she is offering make nonsense of this, since – by offering suitable financial inducements – it is quite possible to persuade doctors to take a course destined to be ultimately fatal to their independence. If she has her way, if the man who agrees to surrender the right to private practice outside working hours is paid a great deal more than his more independent colleague – though for working exactly the same number of hours – and if the latter is compelled to deduct any private earnings from his salary and to accept lower seniority awards, then we have a form of compulsion which is no less stringent for being indirect. Even the full-time consultants see, only too clearly, that if the temptation to receive the financial privileges accorded to the pure in heart is widely accepted, everyone will be drawn down into a bog of bureaucratic ineptitude, that the right of even a minority of consultants to continue in private practice guarantees the freedom of all.

Writing a little later, early in 1976, there are signs of compromise and an uneasy peace may well exist by the time these lines appear. It will not last. Already great inroads have been made into the right of private practice in hospitals; the wholly private sector is under explicit threat without the matter having been submitted to the Royal Commission. The consultants have begun to capitulate. Too plainly, the profession has no chance against the professionals.

But there is far more to all this than the details of a hospital consultant's contract. There is a large and powerful section of the Labour movement that hates and envies the professional standards of the middle classes; and having smashed the doctors, they would proceed to tackle the others. And yet we all know perfectly well, in our hearts, that it is only the punctiliousness with which the middle classes have discharged their professional obligations that has stopped these islands from sinking long ago into the sea. We also know, historically, that wherever the middle class of a country has been destroyed, something far worse from left or right has taken its place. The left wing breeds a hatred and fear of excellence which attacks – sometimes physically – those who, like Professor Eysenck, have the temerity to suggest that genetically determined differences exist in human beings which cannot be regulated by politicians.

It is the old business of levelling down rather than up, of denying something that patently exists and can never be totally suppressed, even under communism – the spirit of emulation and aspiration, the desire to improve the lot of oneself and one's family, to hand on what we have earned to our children, to give them a better start in life. Of course the middle classes have their defects. They are often shortsighted and selfish and greedy and insensitive to the needs of others. Yet these very defects confer a solidity and survival value that are of the greatest importance to the nation, which depends, after all, on enlightened self-interest – the most we can hope to count on. It was Thomas Jefferson who asserted that all men are created equal and independent. The biological variations in physical and intellectual endowment even within one family demonstrate that Jefferson's 'self-evident' truth is a lie. True, we can aim at equality of opportunity, but we can never ensure that the abilities to use these opportunities are equal. Indeed, more opportunity can create – has created – more inequality because it promotes a meritocracy. Hierarchies may founder, social mobility increase, but the percentage of children of industrial workers at the universities is no higher than fifty years ago. No less a person than J. B. S. Haldane, a communist but also a biologist who had to accept the natural diversity of individuals, admitted that the idea of comprehensive education was hopelessly unscientific, flew in the face of biological reality and common sense, and was an immense waste of human possibilities. Great achievement has always rested on effort and standards of perfection – and a fair amount of control. We can rail at and pull down excellence wherever it raises its head; but egalitarianism must lead, and is seen to be leading, to a loutish engineered mediocrity. The trouble is that, as Trotsky said, revolution is a blow at a paralytic; and those of us who dislike what is happening seem to be paralysed before the threat.

If you try too hard to even out advantages conferred by initiative and enterprise, two things will happen: the country will sink into mediocrity, or worse; and the most valuable members of our society will quit these shores for countries where discussion and debate are the prelude, and not the alternative, to decision. This is certainly the case in medicine. Medical emigration to Australia alone has more than doubled in the last twelve months, and it would be naïve to ascribe this flow entirely to greed. While this exodus increases, the gaps in the service are filled by immigrant Asians, and our medical schools continue to deny places to gifted home-bred youngsters and turn out a woefully inadequate supply of doctors every year. And the Department of Health seems prepared to contemplate this situation with complacency. After all, a hospital service in which over half of all the sub-consultant posts are filled by Asians, and an increasing number of all posts by women and the less enterprising, must be more amenable to grandmotherly control. Ah well, to those whom the Gods wish to destroy they first award a social contract.

An important report just published * acknowledges that the NHS

* *Report of the Committee of Inquiry into the Regulations of the Medical Profession.* H.M.S.O., April 1975.

is heavily dependent on overseas doctors whose general competence is undesirably low, because standards have been compromised by the man-power requirements of the service; hence the admission of two or three thousand Asiatics every year. This is the first time that these true but dirty words have been stated officially. They are overdue.

How did this situation arise? It began with a monumental error by the Willink Committee on medical education a good many years back: the decision that we had too many doctors and that the intake of medical schools, which are government-subsidized, should be drastically reduced. Time soon showed that this was wrong; but, as it takes many years to make a doctor, the effects of this error were very long-lasting and cannot be remedied overnight. They were exacerbated by a rising tide of medical emigration, and at the same time the expansion of the NHS increased the number of posts to be filled. The only immediate solution was to import Indian and Pakistani doctors, who already had command of some sort of English and were only too anxious to join the general move westward, though their own countries could have done with their services. (I recall at a conference in Bombay the then President of India begging new graduates to stay and work in the villages. They did not.) I am not going to talk about the advantages and disadvantages of depending so largely on Indian doctors; it has been a historic process in which the needs of both parties have been complementary. Furthermore, I am too fond of my many Indian friends to particularize. (I also remind myself that I am a third-generation immigrant, and think of the time when, bewildered and unhappy, I found written on my locker at medical school the words: 'Bloody foreign Jew'.)

But it seems very wrong that a society like ours should be unable to grow its own doctors. The loss by emigration – and it is considerable – can probably never be made good until we provide greater rewards, and these by no means entirely financial, for enterprise and initiative. But there is also a great loss of talent because places at medical schools are so few that the majority of applicants, many with brilliant school records, have to be turned away. If this situation is allowed to continue, young people will stop coming forward and, as now obtains in the science faculties in the universities, our medical schools will come to count their empty places. Rather late in the day, we are beginning to see the light, but only one or two new schools have been created; there is still no sense of urgency. We could do much better if we began to abandon traditional methods of medical education. Clinical teaching facilities could be multiplied many times, and almost overnight, by making full use of the large district hospitals which cover the country, and attaching them to parent undergraduate centres; many of these already offer postgraduate training. The necessary basis of preliminary science is already fully provided by the schools and polytechnics. The bottle-neck in any expansion is likely to occur in the field of pre-clinical studies in anatomy, physiology and biochemistry; but this could be overcome by a more intensive and imaginative use of existing facilities and by instruction over the air. Everything is possible, if only the will is there. But is it? Or are we condemned to continue our present dolorous shuffle, taking the easy but what is ultimately the hard way; to remain stifled under the blanket of Micawberism the Socialists have flung over us all?

Turning once more to the problems of the health service as a whole. As far as its staff is concerned, the fact that the wage scramble is infectious is not the whole story, or the worst of it. The trouble is that the demands on the service have risen faster than its real resources; and these demands are essentially limitless; an expansion and sophistication of administration is not the answer. Between 1970 and 1973, in England, the number of health service administrators increased by nearly a third. Meanwhile, the working environment of the staff remains painfully inadequate; the antiquated buildings alone tell the story and depress morale. At all levels there is a feeling of impotence under burdensome administration, yet all grades of health workers – even the administrators, for they are harassed too, poor things – must have a considerable and genuine degree of independence if they are to work willingly and happily. The root cause of the difficulties in which consultants find themselves is not really financial. It is a system in which a profession is employed by a government. At present, the Department of Health and Social Security is both ultimate employer and arbitrator, and the politicians are changing the rules as the game proceeds. In sum, a collectivist state-controlled system intended to be free for all is being challenged by both raging inflation and by a profession restive for its independence.

The fact is – and we have all got to recognize this eventually – that there can never be a free, centrally controlled health service equally available to all. It was always a delusion. All we can afford on this basis is the first-class stripped-down service we have had for emergencies only during the period of working to rule. We can only have more than this if the responsibility for medical treatment is handed over – as it should have been originally – to a national health commission or corporation analogous to the BBC and semi-independent of government control, or else to private insurance organizations as in Australia and other countries, the costs removed from the Exchequer to a separately financed basis. Then payment at the time of service, even if subsequently recoverable, would make it plain that medicine costs money. If we had such an independent scheme it might do what has so far not been attempted, i.e. work out agreed priorities, and the State's part would be restricted to administering the arrangements for reimbursing patients' treatment costs.

3

A Chirurgeon must have a strong, stable and
intrepid hand and a mind resolute and mer-
ciless; so that to heal him he taketh in hand,
he be nor moved to make more haste than
the thing requires, or to cut him less than is
needful; but that which does all things as if
he were nothing affected with their cries; not
giving heed to the judgment of the vain
common people who speak ill of Chirur-
geons because of their ignorance.

AMBROISE PARE

The surgeon of today needs attributes not so different from those
listed by Paré four centuries ago. He needs empathy, intuition and
authority; he needs courage and stamina, both mental and physical;
in short, he needs 'heart'. He also needs a moderate degree of intelligence – although he does not have to be over-endowed, it is not an
intellectual trade – a modicum of manual dexterity and a great deal
of common sense. Experience too, but that comes with time. He may
not possess all these qualities to an equal degree; he may excel in
diagnosis and be an indifferent or over-ambitious operator. A fine
technique may the enemy of judgment. But he must know when to
operate and when not to operate, and he must do the right operation
for the right reasons *at the right time*.

Are surgeons born, not made? Some certainly come into the world
destined to wield a scalpel. As far as formal training goes, my impulse
is against it – quite wrongly, for the rational case is overwhelming.
Yet 'training' may be unorganized and unconscious on both sides, and
none the worse for that. I was once complimented on how successfully I had trained my clinic sister – to my great surprise for I had
never given a thought to the matter, merely used her as a working
colleague. But trained she was, and a corresponding asset to the community, for she had been exposed to my methods for ten years.

A great deal is written nowadays about the 'scientific' training of surgeons; but the basic fact is, and always will be, that surgery is learned through apprenticeship, by absorption or osmosis from one's seniors at a very receptive period of life. An authoritative senior can imprint himself as much on a young surgeon as does the first object a fledgling sees after breaking out of the egg. Like individuality itself, surgical practice is an amalgam of assimilations and impressions from outside, containing a growing core of something that is unique. And these impressions may go back further than we know, for we are all conditioned in our professional activities, not only by those who taught us and whom we remember, but by earlier generations whom we never knew. Words and gestures we use in the clinic or operating theatre may once have been the property of a remote surgical ancestor; mannerisms are handed down from our professional for-bears as surely as we genetically inherit the features of our flesh and blood ancestors. So we are all eclectics. I know exactly where I picked up my way of stitching the skin, who taught me the trick of reducing a Colles fracture, and where I borrowed the tone of voice to deal with an hysteric; but a lot of other things just accrued over the years, and some central part of all this is my own.

In the end one develops a personal *style,* a range of views and of things one knows one can do well. Very soon, say by forty or forty-five, this solidifies and ceases to change very much, or it changes only slowly, following the dictum: 'Be not the first by whom the new is tried, nor yet the last to lay the old aside.' One then has a repertoire. And just as a musician will include in his repertoire the pieces he is good at and exclude those in which he doesn't shine, so the finished surgeon will differ from all other surgeons. He won't necessarily be better or worse; but, when there are several options for a given con-dition, it may be wiser for him to do an operation which he does well rather than one intrinsically more suitable for that particular patient. Surgeons know this about each other, and when they or their families need an operation they will choose one man for varicose veins, another to remove a gall-bladder, a third for cancer of the rectum. The ordinary member of the public does not generally have this knowledge, though reputations certainly exist around the consulting areas of London and other cities. And, on the whole, differences between surgeons are measured on this level, rather than in terms of overall competence, though a measure for this certainly exists. One thinks: 'I would prefer A to B for such-and-such an operation,' rather than: 'I would never go to B for anything!'

Basically, I suppose, if one compares an operation to playing a sonata, granting the need for a minimum of manual dexterity, all that matters is that the right notes should be played in the right order. However plodding the performance, the result will be satisfactory: the speed and bravura of execution are of relatively minor importance. You can fly an aeroplane if you follow the book. There are times, at the end of an operation, when I know that no one else in the world could have done it better. There are others when I slink out of the theatre feeling like a criminal bungler. Yet the results, from the patient's point of view, are probably not very dissimilar.

The present-day surgical teacher – and this applies in many fields because things are changing so rapidly – cannot tell his pupils what they are to expect in future times when they are independent practitioners. The most he can do is to encourage an open-minded ability to appraise and respond to novel situations. One of these situations will inevitably be the trend towards computer diagnosis and treatment. Ought this to be resisted? One often knows intuitively and with certainty that a diagnosis is right, before it has been confirmed, in the same way that one knows one will hit the target or that one's letter to *The Times* will be published. But how does one know? It is like St Augustine saying that he knew exactly what time was, so long as no one asked him what it was.

And who will guard the guardians? That is, how can we tell that the training has paid off? The final assessment would have to depend on an appraisal of the efficiency of the trainees when they have become surgeons, and the facilities for this barely exist, or exist only in terms of quantity rather than quality of work. Indeed, the very attempt at such analysis might create a furore. Yet every profession needs to maintain a degree of continuous self-scrutiny, which should have aspects more positive than the mere detection and punishment of negligence or criminality.

There is an apocryphal tale that, in an important medical school noted for the prowess of its football team, the Dean at the selection interview would throw a rugger ball at the candidate. If the candidate missed it, he was failed; if he caught it, he was passed; and if he threw it back, he got a scholarship.

*

The life of a surgeon is often very limited geographically. But he has the advantage of unlimited travel in the field of human experience. He knows what life is about: the heights to which human beings can rise, the depths to which they can sink. Some of the things we see are indescribable, or should not be described. One episode comes to mind. A young woman, totally paralysed by poliomyelitis, lay motionless on a hospital bed month after month without hope of recovery. One day when her husband came to visit her, he removed the wedding ring from her finger. She was unable to prevent him although, without a word being said, she knew that it was to give to another woman. I would not have believed this if I had not seen it.

We all hate those we have injured: because of what we have done to them, because of our feelings of inadequacy and guilt. It would be strange if this were not the case in the surgical relationship. I must admit that I myself dislike many of the patients I've been unable to cure; most surgeons do, though they may be able to disguise this from their patients and often from themselves. Sometimes, in an attempt to retrieve the situation, my sense of failure tempts me into increasingly adventurous procedures, like a gambler doubling his bets. And when these fail, as they occasionally do in this type of case, confusion is worse confounded. In surgery, successive errors cause disability to accumulate at compound interest.

Oddly enough these unsuccessfully treated, damaged or mutilated patients are rarely resentful, in fact they often love their surgeon all the more, as if they had become joined to him in some hazardous enterprise. In my more morbid moments I am reminded of the way a prisoner sometimes forms a close attachment to his gaoler. Often it is those who have had a really difficult technical procedure – which has passed off brilliantly – who take it for granted, offer no thanks, and complain bitterly of the most trivial untoward symptoms.

The degree of identification of a surgeon with his patient is infinitely variable. In consultation he cannot be entirely objective because the patient is another human being: there has to be some empathy, although not too much or it would paralyse his ability to judge and act. But when it comes to the actual operation, total objectivity is essential: what is on the operating table must be a thing; no identification can exist or the operation could not continue. Unconsciously though, and afterwards, the surgeon has to pay a price for temporarily becoming a machine, albeit a sentient one. This is why operating on one's own kin is not a good idea. I have operated on my son, my wife, and one of my mothers-in-law, and the last was the worst.

I should like to quote something from a modern writer, Frederic Raphael, which much appeals to me:

> If medicine allows a man, uniformed in white, to become the therapeutic inquisitor and confessor of his fellow-men, it also exacts a price. The celibacy of the clergy finds its equivalent in the obligatory neutrality of the doctor. He must approach the naked not as a lover, but as a dressed and unerotic Professional Man. He sees others bleed, but he does not bleed for them. . . . If he is professional at the wrong time, he risks an impotence that may humiliate him as a lover. If he is human at the wrong time, he runs the risk of compromising himself with the General Medical Council. . . . The doctor . . . makes a decision to divorce himself from life as others live it.*

The doctor who refers to his patients as males and females instead of as men and women, has taken the first step on the road to Belsen.

The dissociation of surgery: the fact that I am aware of the exact internal structure of a woman's leg does not prevent me from finding some women's legs very attractive.

It is always helpful to make friends of one's patients, dangerous to make patients of one's friends. Complications, financial or emotional, may arise. When Boswell consulted his medical friend Douglas (because he had the clap again), he wrote:

> And here let me make a just and true observation, which is that the same man as a friend and as a surgeon exhibits two very

* From a broadcast talk, reprinted in *The Listener*, 3 April, 1975.

opposite characters. I have to do not with him but with his profession. Douglas as a surgeon will be as ready to keep me long under his hands and as desirous to lay hold of my money as any man.*

As for making love to one's patients, it is remarkable how rarely this happens. Not that one is not tempted at times, but the restraining factor is not so much the thought of the GMC and being struck off, as ordinary propriety. I am told that they order these things better in France.

The surgeon very often has to look a patient in the face – having already seen from his examination and the X-rays that things have gone wrong, or are not going well, or that a condition exists which is beyond treatment – and blandly reassure him that all is well. He must not destroy the other's confidence by allowing himself to express, in voice or feature, a flicker of doubt. This means that he must be insincere; but it is the insincerity of the actor, not the hypocrite. The patient, like the audience, wants to be convinced, is willing to suspend nagging disbelief. This operates particularly with regard to malignant disease. At one level, he does not know and does not want to know. At a deeper level he knows perfectly well. It amazes me how rarely patients ask frankly whether they have cancer, even when I invite the question. And, unlike my American colleagues, I rarely tell them, have done so no more than half a dozen times in thirty years. But sometimes it is necessary: to allow a man to make his last dispositions, or to make peace with himself. I remember one patient who was a roaring nuisance in the ward, alternately bullying and dependent. I judged it wise to inform him of his case; whereupon, his anxieties clarified, he became serene and made a good end.

* *Boswell's London Journal*. Heinemann, 1950.

4

Perhaps this is an appropriate place to wonder why I took up this line of work. To become a doctor was perhaps unavoidable for the son of a middle-class Jewish family. Yet I do not recall that any pressure was ever brought to bear on me, rather the reverse; there was a total lack of guidance in those dreamy adolescent sixth-form days when one's ambitions veered and fluctuated with every fresh influence. I recall wanting, in successive weeks, to be a minister of religion and a tropical parasitologist. But all the time I was sitting for all the scholarships going. I made the fatal and always regretted mistake of declining to wait a year for an offered place at Cambridge (though I eventually came to teach anatomy there as a postgraduate). And under the influence – so it seems to me, yet it could not have been as simple as that – of Francis Brett Young's *The Young Physician*, a splendid book for an embryo doctor, I won a scholarship to University College and University College Hospital. This institution was unique among the London teaching hospitals before the war in having no orthopaedic department as such. The result was that, on leaving, I was dazzled by meeting this entirely new discipline, especially as my first resident post was at the old Royal Free Hospital in the Gray's Inn Road (there were two men among twenty women residents) and my first chief was an orthopaedic surgeon, Paul Jenner Verrall. Verrall was a corpulent Cornishman, a classicist and a disciple of Robert Jones. He was also a member of the Savage Club and used regularly to descend, puffing, from the tram outside the hospital for a clinic or operating session after having reluctantly abandoned a luncheon party at the club. Years, many years, later I was to become a member of the same club; and though I have by now resigned from all the learned societies which so bolster one's ego in the middle years, I am proud to remain a Savage, for the members are the best company in the world. That great and good man, Dr Will Sargant, who treated me so successfully for depression, is also a Savage; our ties betrayed us at my first consultation. At this visit, when I was in dire straits, a strange coincidence emerged. I had under my care at the hospital a very disturbed young man who had slashed his wrist so badly, severing all the nerves and tendons, that the hand threatened to be useless. A very long and complicated operation was in prospect. This man happened also to be a patient of Sargant's. We made an unspoken pact that Sargant would cure me and I would cure the young man; and that is more or less what happened, allowing for the cyclical nature of depression.

But I am off the track. My apprenticeship to Verrall imprinted me with orthopaedics. It is difficult to say exactly where its fascination lies. To begin with, it is the *classical* discipline of surgery, of immense lineage and antiquity, practised long before the more romantic surgery of the body cavities was made possible by anaesthesia and antisepsis (the great gift of anaesthesia to surgery was that it made *leisurely* operating possible). And then, it is a peripheral surgery of the solid parts, the limbs and body-wall and spine, somehow more reassuring than poking about in the abdominal cavity – who knows what one may not find in that gloomy temple of diagnostic humiliation? And it is pre-eminently a field for repair and one which immediately shows the results of repair in improved function. Also, I now feel that there was a real connection with my father's work as a shoe retailer. All of his time was spent in the shop dealing with an endless stream of customers, satisfying their wants and cajoling their indecisions, kneeling with their feet in his hands. For much of my work is to do with feet, and as I sit in my consultant's chair with a patient's foot in my lap, I sometimes wonder whether I have not chosen to repeat my father's story at another level. People often think that orthopaedics is primarily or solely to do with feet. But the word is derived from the Greek *paidos,* a child, not the Latin *pes,* a foot, and was originally devised to express that our discipline is concerned with the straight and proper growth of children, which is still largely the case.

Much of my work is concerned with the management of chronic arthritis – both osteoarthritis and the rheumatoid variety. Sufferers from rheumatoid disease are mostly middle-aged women, and I have often had cause to admire their courage under this cruellest of afflictions. Personally, I would rather have cancer, for there the issue is pretty soon settled one way or the other, whereas rheumatoid arthritis grumbles on, with recurrent flares, for most of a lifetime. These women are always in pain. They wake with pain, pain is their constant companion throughout the day, pain interrupts their sleep. No joint is immune and disability increases until the most everyday actions – grasping, eating, standing, walking – which the rest of us take for granted, become a purgatory. Even modern drugs in large doses do not impose full control; cortisone is the best, but its use carries certain risks. Of course, patients adjust. One can get used to anything. There are merciful and automatic mental mechanisms which contract one's horizons, and the thing is insidious.

So why speak of courage? Because all of us, facing the mirror in the morning, have to ask why we should not hang ourselves today, and these women do not do so. I have had to deal with many women suicides, mostly unsuccessful – and meant to be unsuccessful – but never in a case of rheumatoid arthritis. Theirs is a decision to endure, if just for one day at a time, and this takes the highest form of courage, and no one sees it or knows about it. Once, only once, a talented international civil servant begged me to kill her under the anaesthetic; life had become such a torment. I rallied and teased her, pointed out that she was depressed, that a time would come when this would have passed, which was not easy as I was depressed myself at the time – but that helps one to understand. I did her knee operation, and six months later she was quite a lot better and had retreated temporarily from her despair. But if anyone was entitled to ask for their despatch, she was. Cicero says, 'Remember that the greatest pains are terminated by death. If they be tolerable, we bear them; if not, let us go out of life as from a theatre where the entertainment does not please us.' She had the courage to ask for death and to go on living when I could not grant her request. I constantly marvel at the courage of women.

The position with regard to osteoarthritis, which is shared more equally between the sexes, is different and more hopeful. It is localized to one or two joints, usually the hip or knee, and a great deal can be done surgically, both by the older techniques and by the newer operations for joint replacement with an implant. In the case of the hip this has been a brilliant success, due, I am proud to say, to the unremitting endeavours of one or two British orthopaedic surgeons.

However, I don't really *like* these operations. They are not biological, they do not allow the patient's own tissues to complete the job. The massive inert metal or metal-and-plastic implant which is inserted, is never really accepted and may give trouble as the years pass. However, as most patients are already well on in life, this is not usually very important. I would certainly have it done on myself if the need arose. But, in perspective, I believe that it is a short-term solution and that, in twenty or thirty years' time, we shall have found a simpler and more biological way of controlling the disease process, probably hormonal. After all, arthritis of the hip is very rare in some Asian communities and there must be a reason for this.

This raises the question whether old dogs should learn new tricks, a perpetual problem for the ageing surgeon in a time of rapid technical innovation. My initial reaction to hip replacement was not enthusiastic. I recalled the disasters with plastic replacement of the head of the femur in the 1950s, and preferred to let others try and await the complications. But the popularity of the operation grew, patients began to demand it and to refuse alternative procedures, and what eventually changed my mind were the quizzical looks from young assistants. So I set myself to learn the technique, and now it is probably the commonest of the major operations I do. But I won't do knee replacements, for I recognize the same mental block as when I first came up against the differential calculus – this is not for me – and if a knee replacement seems the right thing to do, I send the patient to a younger colleague.

This sort of problem arises in every field of surgery. There has always been a tendency for the surgeon to regard himself as a complete man, capable of dealing with anything; and in the days when surgeons were much thinner on the ground than now, this was not unreasonable and sometimes even essential. But, in fact, there are bound to be certain fields in which any consultant is not as good as a colleague not so far away. Unfortunately, a blind spot may prevent him from recognizing this and, even if he does, false pride may prevent him from referring a patient. And, because he is immune from criticism, he may not be aware that his work is below par. His colleagues rarely have the opportunity to see his results; his juniors will be aware of the situation but in no position to criticize. This sometimes places a conscientious junior in an intolerable situation. Of course, to some extent, the news gets around eventually, and general practitioners shy off sending certain patients to certain surgeons. A somewhat different problem is the need for a fresh eye when you have been too close to a problem for too long and realize that you are no longer thinking clearly about a patient. That is the time when you should swallow your pride and send him for a second opinion.

The situation becomes much easier when there is a technical field which the surgeon is simply not qualified to tackle. A current example of this is vascular surgery – operations for arterial disease and injury. This is a recent growth and although it is now part and parcel of any surgical training, this has not always been the case. So there are still a number of older surgeons approaching retirement who have to acknowledge that they can't do vascular surgery at all.

Another kind of problem faces the surgeon who is operating under pressure, or who is tired. He may feel that he is expected to be quick or to finish within a certain time to justify his reputation. (The tragedy here is that the gap between a man and his legend tends to widen as time creeps on.) Perhaps someone else is scheduled to use the same theatre immediately after him, or there is an important committee meeting or clinic which he must attend. No surgeon should allow himself to be influenced by such considerations; and if he recognizes them, he should smoke a mental cigarette and slow down.

Then again, it frequently happens in the course of a long list, that one case turns out to be much more difficult and protracted than expected; or perhaps the list may have to be interrupted to deal with a major accident or other emergency. So there you are, much later than you thought, very tired and with one or two patients still waiting for the routine operations which *they* rightly consider to be the most important of the day. Perhaps these patients have already been premedicated. Here, I think, one must have the strength of mind to put off the case until another day, distressing as it may be for a patient who has been waiting and worked-up for hours. But it is in his own interest, and I have never found a patient resentful or ununderstanding in these circumstances.

For the airline pilot, there is a point of no return on take-off. Before this point he can still abort; a moment later he cannot. For the surgeon the point of no return is early; it is when the anaesthetist has inserted his needle into the patient's vein. That is why, in my opinion, it is essential to talk to the patient in the anaesthetic room before he goes under; first, because he will be glad to see you, and to see that it *is* you; second, because you must make sure that you are operating on the right patient, at the right time, for the right condition and on the right side. It is a recurrent terror that one day I shall find the patient already on the table and that the condition diagnosed has disappear-

ed. It happens, but very rarely. And then again, sometimes the patient
will have been put on the waiting-list by an assistant (though I try to
make it a rule to avoid this) and you must check the diagnosis yourself. More than once I have had to send a patient back to the ward
at the last moment, and that is very traumatic to all concerned. I have
to add one episode which is almost unbelievable, but which is indica-
tive of the way we live now. During a union action against private
patients in 1973, two porters were half-way to the theatre with a prepared and premedicated patient when they discovered his private
status and promptly abandoned him on his trolley in the corridor.

5

For it is not sufficient that the Chirurgeon
doe his duty towards the patient, but the
patient must also do his.

AMBROISE PARE

It is not what you do to the patient, but what
the patient does with what you have done to
him.

SIR ARCHIBALD MACINDOE

The British hospital outpatient clinic is, at its most developed, probably unique in world medical practice. Historically, it has more than one origin: the workhouse queues of the poor law, the soup-kitchen, the casualty department, the busy surgeries of general practitioners. Until quite recent times, and to some extent even now, the local hospital in large towns was the traditional resort of transients, the feckless, the drunk and the deranged; of all without a regular doctor of their own. I remember, as a student in the thirties, how whole families would arrive to spend the day in the waiting-hall having their various ills sorted out; how the hospital had its own 'district' for obstetrics, its young men rushing out – always, it seemed, at night – to deliver babies in warrens of slum tenements around King's Cross where, apparently, no daylight or general practitioner ever penetrated. It was, surprisingly, still very much as portrayed at an even earlier epoch by Somerset Maugham in his *Liza of Lambeth*; and the dark tribalism, the foetid poverty, might have been features of a much more primitive society, but they were in the heart of London.

In its origin, the hospital is a charity that goes back to the Middle Ages and before; to a time, indeed, when the hospice or hostel was a refuge without any peculiarly medical connotations. Later, particularly in the eighteenth century, private philanthropy founded the county hospitals that sprang up all over the country – the Royal

Blankshire Infirmary with its elegant columned portico, staffed by the local physicians and surgeons who gave their services for nothing. The foundation and staffing of such a hospital is well described in *Middle-march,* which also hints at the stratification of doctors: the upper-crust physicians who were Fellows of the Royal College of Physicians in London; the lowlier apothecaries; the surgeons, still not quite accepted as proper doctors, operating at the behest of the physician very much as a plumber is called in by a householder. (Emancipation, to the present point when a surgeon may be defined as 'a physician who uses his hands', took a long time.) For the gentry, a doctor was still only a superior kind of servant, and none the worse for that – an attitude that is by no means extinct.

Ideally, one supposes, a hospital clinic should be essentially consultative, with the consultant there simply to give an opinion, to make a diagnosis, to tell the general practitioner how to manage the case. A medical case might require not more than one or two visits; if admission for operation became necessary, supervision might last longer. Something like this used to obtain in the past. But as the *right* to medical care has extended, as hospitals have acquired techniques and laboratories and know-how denied to the GP, as the latter has increasingly come to feel, or been made to feel, that his services cannot compete with those of the institutions, as home visiting declines, as patients demand the superior magic of complicated investigations, so the hospital has increasingly taken over the entire management of many patients, including their births and deaths.

The outpatient clinic, as I have known it, was a fantastic exercise in speed, stamina and professional expertise. I hardly know what to compare it to; possibly the court of a busy London stipendiary magistrate, with its rapid turnover of cases, its rattle of immediate quasi-mechanical decisions, each one affecting the limb, the livelihood, even at times the life of those dealt with. I was once visited in my swarming – and, to be candid, stinking – outpatient clinic at one hospital by a most eminent surgeon, who remarked: 'You don't want a doctor here, you need a machine-gun!'

If you are a proper doctor, the clinic situation creates quite intense feelings of tension and frustration. The sheer volume of work is in itself exhausting; I have seen young doctors, especially women, shaken and white-faced after their first encounters with this ordeal, also quite senior consultants dosing themselves with tranquillizers before going in to bat or to battle. After all, one has been brought up to take a careful history, to make a proper examination, to weigh the evidence, to come to a considered conclusion; and all this takes time. But time is precisely what you have not got in the outpatient department. You are racing against the clock, trying to do something, to establish a relationship, which requires far more time and tenderness than are available, so that you provide only a shadow of the real thing and the patient knows this, and knows that this is all he can hope to get. It is – and I choose the word carefully – a prostitution, for it has exactly the same relation to a genuine medical relationship as sexual prostitution has to a genuine loving relationship. If you have to see fifty, or a hundred, or even more patients at a session, how much care and attention are the last half of these going to get? In a very busy clinic, say a fracture clinic, I tend after a time, in self-defence, to stop looking at the patients and talking to them and glance only at the X-rays and the injured part, a sort of veterinary medicine. It amazes me that we, doctors and patients, have submitted to such an oppressive and inhuman system for so long. One result of recent working to rule has been a reduction in the size of clinics, allowing relaxed and reasonable interviews, hence a determination never to return to the old state of affairs. But we shall have to see; the State will have to pay a great many more doctors to make this possible. At present, many part-time consultants cling on to a tiny private practice simply for the sheer luxury of being able, for a small part of their time, to work under decent conditions; and best of all is the pleasure of looking after sick colleagues or their families. Our slogan should surely be: Every patient a private patient!

If it were not for this unrelenting pressure, outpatient work would be sheer delight. To start with, there are the sensual and intellectual pleasures of diagnosis, the excitement of pursuing a disorder through the confusing dappled light and shade of a forest of symptoms, losing and regaining the trail, often uncertain until the last moment – when you face each other, old friends and foes, over the head of the patient who is to be your battlefield – whether the beast will be easily tamed or stand ferociously at bay. (Admittedly, all is not on this plane; most orthopaedic work is very pedestrian, often literally so.)

Outpatient work is also demanding because, apart from sheer quantity, it is an unequal exchange. The patient hands over his pain and anxiety in exchange for reassurance and treatment. The strain this imposes depends, to some extent, on whether he bears his sufferings nobly or ignobly. Some patients are quite matter-of-fact, but there is usually an aura of unease which may dominate the proceedings. Others behave as if the doctor himself was responsible for their symptoms. Others again – the less curable – use him as a lavatory: not interested in getting better, they want to register their sufferings, to deposit a load of complaint and depart temporarily eased. Having established their *bona fides* as victims, they usually decline, often indignantly, the offer of treatment. There are also those who, by the time the consultant sees them, have completely recovered from the condition for which their doctor wrote his letter a few weeks earlier. They come because they can't deny themselves the *bon-bon* of a hospital visit, protest that they 'feel like a fraud' and that is exactly what they are – time-wasting frauds. Then there are those, described by the great French neurologist Charcot as *les malades au petit bout de papier,* who come with their symptoms, particularly their bowel habit, carefully written down on the back of a postcard. There are also the truculent and litigious, who remind the orthopaedic surgeon that bones are filled, not with red marrow, but with black ingratitude.

Orthopaedic patients are, almost by definition, particularly trying because they are neurotic, or of poorer moral fibre, than the generality of persons. They are less able to tolerate the aches and pains that the healthier in spirit make light of. Two persons may have identical conditions but only one will think of coming to hospital, and this is because his threshold of discomfort has been lowered by emotional upset or depression, or the discontent magnified by neurosis. When the condition has obviously been present for many years, the operative question is 'Why have you come now?'

Many patients simply find it a benefit to report regularly to some impersonal unmoving figure. They seem to want to test him, to find with relief that they cannot infect him with their own hysteria. For these an idol would probably do as well, or a peculiarly-shaped stone, or perhaps a tape-recorder. Again, in many cases of chronic illness, the sufferer is using his disease as a weapon against society, a marriage-partner, even against himself, with the surgeon as an unwilling accomplice. Frequently, in fact usually, a patient will take his discharge at the termination of some complicated and highly successful procedure without a word of thanks. Not that I mind this; for the patient to dismiss the doctor with the disease is one index of cure.

Dependence is the last item to be dissolved. Then there are those maddening individuals of whom Montaigne wrote: 'He who has neither the courage to die nor the heart to live, who will neither resist nor fly, what can we do with him?' But then, most patients are frightened: because they are in a strange place and the surgeon is on his home ground; because they don't speak the language and he does; because they are undressed and he is dressed (or fancy-dressed); because they are lying down and he is standing up. They also know that, when he says 'I am afraid we are going to have to operate,' he means '*You* are afraid we are going to have to operate.' I try to minimize all this as much as possible; by never wearing a white coat, by getting rid of the other-side-of-the-desk situation, by speaking colloquially.

In all these relationships the patients are replenished from the surgeon's own limited store of optimism and reassurance, and he is left with a deposit of their insecurity and depression. And when his store is exhausted, to whom can *he* turn for revitalization? A woman once said to me: 'Thank God you are always here to look after us!' I said under my breath: 'Yes, but who is going to look after *me*?'

And as evening comes, at the end of the work, the Yahoos dispersed, bespattered with the day's ordure, he is fit for nothing but an enormous drink *pour chasser la honte du jour*.

6

The problem of priorities in treatment when resources are limited. At present, one accords priority to those in great pain, to those who are disabled but capable of repair, to patients with malignant disease, to life-threatening emergencies, always to children. (Also, to be honest, to those one *likes*.) But these decisions are made on the basis of individual suffering and need; they are not necessarily consistent with the good of the country as a whole. It might be argued that we are becoming a too compassionate society, and that in our zeal for the poor and aged we overlook the fact that everything rests on our industrial production and solvency. In which case our most urgent medical task is to get youngish men and women back on their feet and into the factory as quickly as possible. And, in fact, in the classical two-party clinical situation there is now, and increasingly, an unseen third party – the State. The State cannot be excluded from the consulting-room because the aims of surgery include not only the patient's life and the quality of that life, but also his capacity to work.

I suppose every surgeon has his own scale of priorities; and it must be acknowledged that fortunately, so far, administration has never interfered with clinical decisions. We do have some experience, however, of priorities based on the general rather than the individual need. On the battlefield, after an air-raid or an IRA outrage, one accords priority, if facilities are overstretched, to those who are most likely to survive – the young, the not too gravely wounded. Those who are so terribly wounded that even heroic surgical endeavour is unlikely to save them must be left till last if there aren't enough surgeons or blood to go round, for one can do more good more profitably for half a dozen others in the same time. In famine, you allocate the food you have to those who are least seriously affected because they have the best chance of survival. The others must be left to die.

Even so, in ordinary life there is a potential conflict between the interests of the patient and those of the State. Where surgery is concerned, we have the waiting-list. I never think of those on it as divided into the productive and the non-productive. Should I? The injured

119

are necessarily admitted as emergencies; but an old woman never free from the pain of an arthritic hip and unable to sleep or walk may be kept waiting for years for lack of a bed. Is her need any less? As an orthopaedic surgeon, my spurs to action are: first, pain, and close behind, loss of function that I know I can remedy. Malignant disease also attracts attention, rather because of its nature than because one can be sure of doing any good.

The waiting-list does, as I say elsewhere, have the function of allowing some patients to recover without treatment, so preventing unnecessary surgical interference. It also conceals a mass of suffering, patiently borne. And this is mostly reserved for women, because women outlive their husbands and the women's wards are full of old ladies who will never go home again, even if the original reason for admission was a trivial one. Many of these have had hip fractures. Recovery may or may not be complete, but in the meantime the home has broken up, the relatives with a growing family in a three-bedroomed suburban house who have at last got rid of grandma have no intention of ever having her back again. And time passes, and the poor creatures become institutionalized; they pass the critical point when they lose their capacity for independence, and sometimes the will to live. They are well enough looked after, their hair tied with ribbons, but as animated dolls. The country's hospitals are full of them, and it is their presence that so denies and delays treatment for younger and socially more useful members of society. And the acres and acres of geriatric beds, the largest single hospital specialty! The drooling demented creatures whose preservation makes one think shudderingly of those terribly wrong lines: 'Grow old along with me/ The best is yet to be'! We never had these before the war. Where were all these old persons then? In municipal hospitals? In workhouses? Still in the bosom of caring families?

I feel very gloomy about all this. If I were an administrator, I would make an almighty effort to get these patients out of hospital altogether – into hostels, halfway houses which did not demand expert surgical or nursing skills, leaving the wards free for their proper activities.

As for the old ladies with broken hips, they should be regarded as requiring operation as urgently as patients with perforated ulcers. They should be rushed from the receiving room to the theatre and receive a sufficient concentration of nursing attention and physiotherapy to get them on their feet immediately, for every hour counts. But this does not happen. Too often they are allowed to linger in bed for days because scheduled operating lists must not be interrupted or because the anaesthetist thinks their condition is too poor for operation. (It always gets worse.) The procedure of pinning the fracture is nearly always done by an Indian assistant and not by the consultant. This is not a bad thing, because the Indian can usually do it better; but it is a pity that many a young Asiatic surgeon leaves these shores after a stay of some years having had, as his major experience, the pinning of hip fractures that most of us find various reasons for not doing ourselves. It was not always so. I take my share of the blame. I did my best when I was younger, sometimes doing as many as six of these operations in an afternoon. But the supply is unending, and *j'ai perdu ma force et ma gaieté*. It would not be strange if the ultimate solution proved to be biological, for there are many parts of the world where old ladies do not break their hips, and perhaps one day a simple dietetic or hormone supplement for women after the menopause will stop their bones from softening.

Part of the trouble is the way we organize our orthopaedic services. We do have a number of excellent orthopaedic institutions, usually linked with university hospitals. But most orthopaedic work is still carried on in penny packets of wards, or parts of wards, housed in general hospitals and struggling with other departments for facilities. This is all wrong. Taking London, we ought to divide it into a few geographical sectors and give each sector not more than one or two independent orthopaedic units in which to concentrate the scarce skills of orthopaedic surgeons, nurses and physiotherapists. We might even have occupational therapists – I haven't set eyes on one for years. There would be difficulties; patients and relatives would have to travel longer distances. But it would be worth it. And it would have the advantage that individual orthopaedic surgeons would no longer have to work in such relative isolation from each other. We have not gone as far as the neurological and thoracic surgeons in concentrating our services. The general surgery, or most of it, could be left at the periphery.

Another aspect of the matter, which may be a little difficult to explain to the layman, is the difference between orthopaedic and traumatic surgery. Historically, orthopaedics was concerned with the management of deformities, particularly in children, with skeletal defects and disorders which evolve slowly and whose care is a matter of months or years. Traumatic surgery, on the other hand, has to do with fractures and other injuries which must be treated immediately, and in which we can often achieve a rapid restoration to normal. Now, because both disciplines deal with the same structures – bone, muscle, tendons and nerves – it is usually accepted that both should be practised by the same individual. This is the official view. But it is not mine. I see the two as so different in tempo and approach as to need quite different kinds of therapist; and I would like to see this division recognized also in terms of hospital wards, for it is not encouraging for long-term orthopaedic patients to see the injured recovering comparatively quickly and returning to the outside world. I do not disguise the fact that I do not really *like* treating fractures, though I do so. The complicated repair jobs often required are not my style. (I much prefer what my American friends call 'ashcan surgery', the removal rather than the repair of a part. It is surprising what the human body can do without. If the collar-bone does not unite after a fracture you can take it out and throw it away; the cosmetic and functional result is excellent.) If orthopaedic services were concentrated as I suggest, it would be possible to segregate the injured from those with arthritis or deformity, and to allow surgeons to follow their individual bent either in classical orthopaedics or in trauma.

7

'The act of killing and destroying a man'
continued my father, raising his voice and
turning to my uncle Toby – 'you see is glorious and the weapons are honourable!'

LAURENCE STERNE, *Tristram Shandy*

'Then the camps of the wounded – O
heavens, what scene is this? – is this indeed
humanity – these butchers' shambles?'

WALT WHITMAN

War has always given a great fillip to the development of surgery;
but that subject is too vast to develop here. My own service in the
RAMC during the Second German War was spent entirely in a military hospital on the edge of Dartmoor, where the wounded were only
seen long after the event. But I have had first-hand experience of war-
wounds under widely varying circumstances.

At the outbreak of the war the civil authorities believed that air-
raids would cause an enormous number of casualties, which might
overwhelm the existing hospital facilities. To meet this need a
number of hospital sectors were designated in the London area, with
central institutions linked to peripheral and rural base hospitals.
There was rapid improvisation. Much use was made of fever hospitals
and of newly-erected hutted hospitals attached to old workhouse
facilities. Young surgeons – or even, as in my case, would-be surgeons
still studying for the Fellowship of the Royal College of Surgeons –
were whipped away from their classes and planted at strategic points.
But no one really knew what to expect.

I was initially posted to a fever hospital in the East End. There was
almost nothing to do. But one day, in the winter of 1939, a young
married woman was admitted, desperately ill after having aborted
herself, or having been aborted. She was severely shocked – clay-

123

coloured, half-conscious – with peritonitis and septicaemia, and this was before the days of antibiotics. I opened her abdomen and found the uterus rotten and stinking; it had been perforated by an instrument. The only course seemed to be to remove it, but a hysterectomy under such circumstances was very hazardous. However, it was done, the girl became increasingly shocked, and she died as the last stitches were being inserted, with the table tilted steeply to drain as much blood as possible to her head.

I had never done this operation before, though I knew what to do. Although it was necessary, and done adequately, when it was all over I felt like a murderer. Utterly exhausted, I took the Tube home for it was my evening off. The train was brightly lit and full of passengers who did not share my concern and my grief. And when I got home, it was to find the family cosy and chattering round the fire. My entry caused some badinage. 'Where have you been? Cutting someone up?' I was unable to speak.

A little later we moved to Epping. This was near an airfield and also on one of the routes used by incoming bombers; so, after Dunkirk, air-raid casualties began to flow in. The area was full of evacuees and a local institution had been converted into a hostel for expectant mothers. One night a land-mine exploded nearby, and a dozen women were brought in with terrible and identical injuries. They were all East-Enders, built like horses, and their buttocks had been blown off. We worked through the night; with the fatigue and the glassy unreality of it all, it seemed like a dream, like being bound to the wheel of life and death. The technical problems were fascinating; the human problems had to be kept at arm's length. Moreover, the crimson wounds, set against the brown iodine-stained skin, were curiously beautiful; I understood why the Chinese call a wound a 'blossom'. And all through that night the lady I had just married, a senior student at the Royal Free Hospital, was posted with a scalpel in a ghastly vigil in the ward where the injured women lay, prepared instantly to rip the baby from the belly of any woman who died.

Later still, I transferred to Stoke Mandeville Hospital at Aylesbury, then functioning in part as an auxiliary hospital for the Royal Navy. Because of this we received a trainload of wounded after the Dieppe raid. These men had had field-dressings and morphia and nothing else. They were grimy, shocked, some terribly wounded; none complained. We operated for the best part of twenty-four hours, with

hort breaks for rest and refreshment. Only one case now stays in my
memory – a Canadian with gas-gangrene from a thigh wound, who
had to be amputated at the hip to save his life. A few years later, with
the help of antibiotics, we might have saved his leg. Later still, with
the advent of the high-pressure oxygen chamber, we could certainly
have done so. It is important to have one's injuries or illnesses at the
right time.

During the war also, I had to deal with a soldier who had been
wounded above the collar-bone. The nerves to the arm were paralysed; and worse, much worse, the great artery and vein of the limb
had been opened into each other and formed a pulsating aneurismal
mass the size of a fives-ball. This was beyond me and, I thought, perhaps beyond anyone, for no one could tackle this with the certainty
of preserving the limb. I handed the case over to an older surgeon I
much admired, a devout Christian, at another hospital. The operation, at which I assisted, took seven hours. We started by dividing the
clavicle to gain access, and were confronted with an evil throbbing
fibrous mass. It was now apparent that one false step could mean,
not just the loss of the arm, but that of the patient as well. For hours
S. patiently and courageously worked away at this monster, isolating
and defining the great vessels and the false passage between them and
the aneurismal sac itself. After four hours of this he stopped work
suddenly and stood stock-still for a few minutes with his head bowed.
This puzzled me at the time; later I realized that he had been praying.
And it worked. This was a case which many would have regarded as
inoperable from the first, or abandoned half-way through. S. completed it magnificently.

In the years after the war really serious injuries only dribbled in
irregularly, after traffic accidents. (We seem to be willing, as a nation,
to continue to accept the sacrifice of the lives of several thousand
children every year in order that the traffic may continue to roll.)
There were one or two railway accidents with scores of injured. But
I saw nothing comparable to the injuries of the war until the IRA
began their murderous bombing campaign in England thirty years
later. My main feeling then, after one terrible night, was one of indig-
nation: to be thrust back to the beginning again, to have to deal with
surgical problems one had thought extinct. This senseless, wanton,
random killing was like that of the air-raids; and, once again, the

wounded did not complain, were less indignant than myself. I have to add that the energy and selflessness of every member of the hospital staff on this occasion were outstanding; indeed, the prevailing atmosphere – and the word is used precisely – was one of *gaiety*. (The next morning we were back to our usual atmosphere of grumbling dissatisfaction.)

At the end of the night I was unable to sleep and, by a strange coincidence, the first book I opened was one of Thackeray's which contained these remarks addressed to an Irish colleague a century ago:

> Let a Saxon beseech you to hold your hand before you begin this terrible sport. . . . Do the English answer you with a hundredth part of the ferocity with which you appeal to them? Do they fling back hatred for your hatred? Do they not forget their anger in regard for your misery, and receive your mad curses and outcries with an almost curious pitying forbearance? *Now,* at least, the wrong is not on our side, whatever in former days it may have been.

I thought also of that great and compassionate French military surgeon, Ambroise Paré. This passage describes an episode from the expedition against Turin in 1537:

> We entered the throng in the Citty and passed over the dead bodyes, and some which were not yet dead; we heard them cry under our horses' feet, which made my heart relent to leave them. . . . I entered into a stable . . . where I found foure dead souldiers, and three which were leaning against the wall, their faces wholly disfigured, and neither saw nor heard, nor spoake; and their cloathes did yet flame with the gunpowder which had burnt them. . . . There happened to come in an old souldier, who asked me if there were any possible meanes to cure them, I told him no; he presently approached them, and gently cut their throates without choler. Seeing this great cruelty, I told him he was a wicked man, he answered me that he prayed to God that whensoever he should be in such a case, that he might finde someone that would doe as much for him, to the end he might not miserably languish.

Who can read this without a contraction of the heart? What can one say more of war?

8

Treatment makes the therapist feel good.

ANON

A defence of conservatism in treatment is no more – and no less – than the recognition of natural method in healing. We have the old aphorism that if an assistant does not think his chief is too conservative, there is something wrong with the assistant, or the chief, or both. But I also want to mount an attack on over-active surgical interference and on the concept of 'scientific medicine' – a contradiction in terms, for medicine is an art and not a science, or at most a bridge between the two. Like the creative arts, medical practice draws deeply on the unconscious. A one-sided polemic may appear to caricature the truth; but there is an underlying truth to be caricatured. One need not forget the brilliant achievements of modern surgery; but such achievements should not close our eyes to the basis of natural law we rest on. And yet, if we are not careful, each increase in knowledge leads to a narrowing of attention and a loss of perspective. A multiplicity of specialists does not add up to a complete human being; yet only a human being can really handle sickness in another individual. And if I take my critical examples from orthopaedic practice, the argument applies, *mutatis mutandis,* to the other surgical disciplines as well.

The following quotation from the *Last Poems* of D. H. Lawrence comes suitably to hand :

> I am not a mechanism, an assembly of various sections,
> And it is not because the mechanism is working wrongly that I
> am ill.

Words that might well be graven over the portals of our hospitals.

The human body is not entirely a machine; it is more than the sum of its parts, possesses its own wisdom in self-repair, and any form of

127

treatment which ignores this does so at its peril.

Unfortunately, orthopaedic surgery, *par excellence,* lends itself to such narrow misinterpretation. The very nature of the skeleton – its parts and levers, and the muscles which move them – invite us to think in terms of the carpenter's bench. The contents of our journals are too often reminiscent of a plumber's catalogue. This is particularly true of fracture treatment, especially in North America; yet this 'we can fix it' approach is a long step, in time and temper, from the teaching of our forbears.

The spiritual ancestor of present-day British orthopaedic surgeons, the man who laid down the principles of our art in the mid-nineteenth century, was an eccentric Welshman – himself a doctor but the last of a long line of unqualified bone-setters – Hugh Owen Thomas. He practised in Liverpool, where he worked for thirty years, seven days a week, without a holiday. He taught that the body can look after itself very well if we give nature the chance, and that our major task is to provide the rest – local and general – that she needs to get on with the job: 'Rest enforced, uninterrupted and prolonged.' Thomas stressed the importance of efficient rigid splintage of fractures and diseased joints in functional position. He operated when necessary, but insisted that operation was only an incidental means to securing proper rest. Unfortunately he was a very prickly prophet, and unsparing in castigating those who thought they could cajole or force nature into their own mould. He was ostracized by the medical profession and never held a hospital appointment, and his books were unread; but the people of Liverpool stopped work on the day of his funeral.

A lucky accident saw to it that Thomas's work did not die with him. This accident lay in his having adopted as apprentice his wife's nephew, Robert Jones, a great-hearted man as suave and persuasive as Thomas had been polemic. Jones made his reputation in treating the many casualties which accompanied the building of the Manchester Ship Canal, and he had no difficulty in securing hospital posts and spreading the orthopaedic gospel. In the First World War he inspired the enormous expansion of orthopaedic surgery and saved thousands of lives at the front by introducing Thomas's own splint for the management of gun-shot fractures of the thigh-bone. Jones, in sum, made Thomas's principles acceptable to the profession as their originator could never have done. The catalogue of orthopaedic surgeons is a long one in time and space; but it was Thomas who ushered in the modern era and Jones who laid down, in Shropshire and North Wales, the pattern for all subsequent orthopaedic services – a specialized central hospital linked with a number of outlying clinics.

Jones trained many pupils and particularly left his stamp on G. R. Girdlestone who, during that war, set up a centre for the wounded at Oxford, which developed into the Wingfield-Morris Orthopaedic Hospital and is now the Nuffield Orthopaedic Centre. At the height of his powers, Girdlestone was one of the greatest of all orthopaedic surgeons – a brilliant operator, warm-hearted and generous, very religious, but, like Thomas, scathingly critical of inefficiency in treatment, which, on occasion, would rouse him to great anger. I well recall the scarlet faces of some very eminent members of our craft after a dressing-down in front of the patient. But he was of great underlying modesty; and he once wrote to me as an obscure registrar after some brilliant and intricate operation he had devised for the tendons of the foot: 'I have done my small part, now it is up to you to do the major part – educate, animate, rehabilitate !' These are things that stick in the minds of young men.

How much more accurate the older terms for surgical operations were: surgical intervention; better still, surgical interference. These are good words because they describe the essentially *wanton* nature of a deliberate surgical procedure – where the decision to operate is one of choice and not of necessity. The danger of the elective operation – and most operations are elective – is that it is the prime cause of iatrogenic disease – disease created by the physician. Of all our activities, orthopaedics is more potent than most in its ability to initiate such disorders, for we have it in our power to burn, damage, kill and generally insult bone as never before. And bone, like the elephant, never forgets an injury. One false step may lead to a lifetime clouded and crippled by complications. Recurrent flares of infection, non-union, amputation – these are some of the possibilities; and they are less rare than we like to think, in spite of antibiotics. So that we may find ourselves having to treat, not the original lesion, but the ill-consequences of treatment (or the consequences of ill-treatment); as Thomas put it, to find remedies for the remedy, rather than the disease itself. Many surgical mistakes on soft tissue can be put right fairly easily; this is not the case with bone.

What then are the sources of this therapeutic drive, which may at times have such dire results? Let us now examine some of the factors that motivate what we can only call, on occasion, the *furor therapeuticus*.

'Brute force and bloody ignorance'

This is the classic comment of a general surgeon who sees an orthopaedic colleague struggling to reduce a fracture under imperfect anaesthesia. But perhaps there is such a type, for I recall a candidate for a post offering a testimonial which stated blandly that 'Mr X. has been responsible for most of the trauma in this hospital.'

Arrogance, ignorance and stupidity

Of these *arrogance* is the worse fault – the idea that, when something is wrong, the surgeon steps in as *deus ex machina* to put everything right with a stroke of the scalpel. It is an attitude basically contemptuous of the natural history of disease and the natural methods of healing, an attitude that regards the human body as nothing more than a watch, with no self-repairing capacity of its own. It is an attitude ignorant of the fact that patients adapt to their diseases, and diseases to their patients, to reach a symbiosis which is often remarkably durable and efficient. Where a machine will falter or grind to a standstill, a man, because he has a heart and a brain, can often make a remarkable adjustment to even very severe disability.

This is especially so with congenital deformities, or disorders such as spastic paralysis. Life is difficult for these patients, but it is *their* life; they make the best of their limited powers. The surgical treatment of spasticity is too often based on the arrogant assumption that the abnormal must be made normal by dividing nerves and tendons or fixing joints, ignoring the fact that the pathways established in the central nervous systems of these patients since infancy correspond exactly to their spastic state. All their co-ordination is based on this and it is not surprising that the sudden surgical undermining of their structural basis, after years of habituation, may have disastrous results. Patients who could run may now be able only to walk, and those who could walk may be reduced to sitting down, despite the fact that their deformities have been beautifully corrected. Surgery without rehabilitation is worse than useless; and if retraining is thorough, surgery is needed only for carefully selected patients.

The same remarks apply to patients with chronic arthritis, who adapt themselves in a manner which should not be disturbed so long as it is stable. It is unfortunate that decisions to operate are so often made out of sheer despair; failure can often be predicted when the surgeon gives way to repeated pleas in a busy clinic. Impatience is not an indication for intervention. If despair *is* to be an indication, let it be the despair of the patient, for then the surgeon is on a very sound psychological wicket. A great surgeon used to say: 'The right time to operate for osteoarthritis of the hip is when the patient comes, cap in hand, and says: "For Gawd's sake do something, Guvnor, I can't stand it no longer!" '

Coupled with arrogance, and indeed its inevitable corollary, is *ignorance*: ignorance of the natural history of disease. If we interfere prematurely, or unnecessarily, we deprive ourselves of the opportunity of studying the natural history of a disorder, its evolution and decline, and this is an important part of our knowledge. We may even *prevent* natural recovery by our efforts. It is disheartening to see young residents switch from one antibiotic to another when an ice-pack would do as well, or a case failing to respond because a collection of pus is clamouring to be let out. Most non-fatal conditions – such as the low back-aches, the sciaticas, the brachial neuralgias – have their own curve of onset and spontaneous recovery, so that any remedy applied at the apex of the curve gains the credit. We ought to be familiar with all this before impertinently offering treatment which may prolong or complicate recovery. We have so many new weapons, the tempo of life is so fast and the demands for rapid cure so clamant, that we are losing the perspective, balance and restraint which a sound knowledge of untreated disease would give us.

But one unexpected gain on the roundabouts comes from the chronic shortage of beds in our health service. In reviewing long waiting-lists, one is surprised to find that many lesions normally regarded as requiring operation, have either resolved or obviously need no treatment. It makes one wonder whether the expansion of hospital services, for which there is so much outcry, would be an unmixed blessing. Delay does at least give some patients the chance to get better before we can get at them. Perhaps the most valuable remark we can write on a case-sheet is 'Leave alone'. Unfortunately, this does not apply to outpatient clinics where, every day, we busily deny ourselves the knowledge that the most painful shoulders and troublesome tennis elbows always recover completely, even if untreated.

A wise old physician, after listening patiently to the multifarious forms of treatment advised by his students at the bedside, used to say quietly at the end: 'But what will happen, gentlemen, if we do nothing?' It seems important that we should know the answer to this before we do something.

Allied to this is ignorance of a proper analysis of *causation* in treatment. I do not refer to the simple *post hoc, propter hoc* fallacy, though this is always important. I mean that success in treatment may follow from something quite other than what we think we are doing. Cynics speak of 'the inevitable 70 per cent' of cures in any operation for any non-fatal condition, for a great many things happen in even the simplest procedures. Thus, before the war, success often attended destructive procedures on perfectly innocent joints in the low back for sciatica, which we now know to be due to a prolapsed intervertebral disc. But consider what happened to these patients.

They entered into a therapeutic relationship with the surgeon. They had an operation under a general anaesthetic. This was followed by reparative processes and by prolonged recumbency and physiotherapy. The variables are so many that it is impossible to postulate with certainty that the popular operation of the time was the agent of cure. It is not cynicism to take a long cool look at what happens when we do things to patients. Thus, it is an empirical fact that manipulation of the spine under anaesthesia can be an excellent treatment for low back-ache and sciatica: if it were not so, unqualified manipulators would not be in such demand. But once more there is the therapeutic situation. And there is the anaesthetic, which may be very important. Many of these patients, especially housewives, are tense, harried and exhausted, and the temporary oblivion and relaxation of deep anaesthesia does them the world of good. I am not arguing that the manipulation in itself is of no value, only that you cannot possibly tell without a control series where half the patients are anaesthetized but *not* manipulated. It might be illuminating if we had the courage to run such a series.

A propos of *stupidity*, it has always seemed to me to be an excellent thing for a surgeon to be lazy, for if he is lazy and stupid the damage he can do is far less than if he is stupid and energetic; while an intelligent but energetic surgeon is often tempted into operating for the sheer technical pleasure of exercising his skill, and so runs corresponding risks. I would always back the lazy, intelligent man who never operates unless it is really necessary; who, at perhaps five minutes to twelve, makes just that intervention required to save a life or change the course of a disease.

Missionary reparative zeal

There is no need to say much about this. It is laudable, admirable and essential. It is what we start with and what keeps us going, and he is a sad man whose work it does not flavour. But it must not lead us into any of the pitfalls under discussion.

Perfectionism

Beware the surgeon who acts out with his patients an unending quest for the ideal, actuated primarily by inner motives and not by the real needs of the case. It is pre-eminently this type who, in his dissatisfaction with the merely competent result, creates iatrogenic disease, and who seeks endless improvement in successive procedures. Of him it is true that *le mieux est l'ennemi du bien*, for in his pursuit of the best the merely good is trampled underfoot. Is life so long, is our art so strong, that we can waste our patients' time and our own energies because we are satisfied only with perfection? Surely this is to overlook the basic adaptability of humanity, the healthy mediocrity on which everything rests.

On the other hand, it is only fair to note the opposite danger, that of therapeutic nihilism, which may also be a matter of temperament. If we hesitate too long, we may be unable to act at all. Intelligence is not always a surgical virtue. Too much clarity and objectivity, too analytical an awareness of all the factors involved, may abolish just that blinkered self-confidence and enthusiasm which are half of cure. And patients instinctively resent objective enquiry by the surgeon. I have often asked my own patients bluntly whether they thought that my operations had done them any good, only to excite feelings as outraged as if I had made an indecent proposal. My enquiry was obviously improper in their view, for it was important to them that, *qua* therapist, I should have no doubts at all that my treatment was beneficial.

This is why a surgeon whose technique is less than perfect, but who fully and instinctively understands the art of giving himself to the patient, often gets better overall results than a much more accomplished but unsympathetic technician. We should not altogether deprive ourselves, through excessive self-scrutiny, of the personal magic which is so important at a time when we are increasingly called on to fill what Julian Huxley called 'the God-shaped blank' that science has created in modern society. Patients need this magic. Doctors need it when they become patients. Of course, science is magical too. There is the magic of the machine, of the X-ray and the Geiger counter, but this is expensive. Personal magic is cheaper and lasts longer, and we always have to return to it in the end.

The Aesthetic Fallacy

This is a much more amiable sin. One of the most impressive features of the human body is the beauty and accuracy of its construction and its natural symmetry. In the developing foetus, different organs mature in synchronous reciprocal growth. In the young child the limbs and parts mirror each other exactly and reach identical lengths at identical times. In the adult skeleton there is the marvellous correspondence of the two halves of the pelvis and of the shafts of the long bones. If a machine were to accomplish all this, we should call it a miracle of ingenuity.

But Nature only performs this miracle once. If an organ or tissue is breached, it is repaired only by a fibrous scar. Nature is content with a sound, rough job. The only exception – where the bridging tissue repeats the original pattern – is, oddly enough, in bone. And when the gross pattern of the skeleton is disrupted by injury it is never, at least in adult life, restored. Adjustment, not renewal, is the rule. But, because modern technique gives us the power to do what Nature does not even try to do, we may allow aesthetic compulsions to lead us to restorative procedures carrying no little risk. Here are two examples.

A disruption of the pelvis seems to be crying out for operative reduction. The surgeon in charge resists that temptation and the patient, a gymnast and track runner, is running and jumping again within eight weeks. This result could not possibly have been bettered by operation; but the patient could have been made very much worse, for some of these cases are operated on and a proportion develop complications. What a contrast between a demoralized patient rotting in bed week after week, and one treated by ignoring the X-rays and getting on with rehabilitation! It is the old contrast between 'what

might have been and what is but hadn't ought to be', as Bret Harte
says in one of his ballads. And it is due to the drive to restore Nature's
symmetry when she herself would not have bothered, and to the surgeon's inability to resist this drive.

Again, in a fracture of the upper end of the shin-bone the bone is
shattered to fragments and this excites a powerful impulse in the
surgeon to recreate the original design. But from the merely practical
viewpoint, the more shattered the bone the more certain is union,
since such a large raw surface is exposed. This fracture cannot be
prevented from uniting except by quite extraordinary exertions on
the part of the surgeon. And as union is certain, and as length and
alignment can readily be maintained by traction and splintage, what
reason can there be for operation? It can only be an aesthetic one.
The therapist is overcome by the X-ray appearances and treats these
instead of the patient of whom they are but a shadow. In one such
case an operation was done (*mea culpa!*), the X-ray appearances were
delightfully improved, but infection occurred and the patient spent
the subsequent years with recurrent flares of infection, underwent
many operations, and was always under the threat of amputation. He
had been a happy, jovial man, a docker near retiring age, and he lost
his job, his peace of mind, and much of his pension. It was (you may
agree) rather a high price to pay for a good-looking X-ray.

And this is by no means an exceptional case. There are many who
advocate routine open operations on fractures on the grounds that
this removes uncertainty about the accuracy of reduction and fixation
and shortens hospital stay, and that infection occurs in perhaps only
one per cent of cases. Well, we know that the answer we are likely to
get, when hot for certainty in surgical life, is a dusty one. Shortening
of stay in hospital should never be an indication for an operation that
is not strictly necessary. Even one failure, with all the invalidism this
may imply, is not compensated by the ninety and nine which are
successful. It is true that the violence of modern life creates certain
fractures which can *only* be dealt with by operation. The motorcycle
is responsible for fractures of the thigh-bone which cannot be reduced
and cannot unite unless they are operated on, so driven into the
muscles are the fragments; and in fractures of this kind. operation is
brilliantly successful. But this does not mean that every fracture of the
thigh-bone in an adult should be nailed; and yet this is exactly the
position that obtains in many hospitals because nurses and residents

no longer have the time and skill to manage these cases by splintage, and because the pressure of waiting-lists demands a rapid turnover. It is a very serious state of affairs when the indications for an operation like this cease to be purely clinical and become determined by social and administrative factors. The more so when our overcrowded wards, with their harried staffs and deteriorating standards, become reservoirs of resistant bacteria so that, in some places and at some times of the year, it is about as safe to operate from them as in a public sewer.

Surgical Bovarism

Akin to, but not the same as perfectionism, is 'Surgical Bovarism', a phrase I have coined to describe a surgical attitude, well illustrated in Flaubert's *Madame Bovary,* which tends to force operations on to afflicted but well-adjusted individuals. There is an episode in the novel that perfectly displays the wanton nature of such interference and its possible dire results. The village chemist, who had read of a marvellous new treatment for club-foot, induced Emma to persuade her husband to operate on the local ostler. 'What risk is there?' he asked. . . . 'Success, practically certain. An end of suffering and disfigurement for the patient. Immediate fame for the operator. Why shouldn't your husband operate on poor old Hippolyte . . . and what's to prevent me sending a little paragraph to the paper about it?' Charles let himself be persuaded and, while he was studying the technique and which tendon to cut, all manner of arguments were used to induce Hippolyte to submit to the operation. 'The poor fellow gave in, for . . . everyone from the Mayor down, urged and shamed and lectured him. But the decisive factor was that it *wouldn't cost him anything.*'

You know the sequel. The operation went off well enough, but the leg became gangrenous and a more experienced surgeon had to amputate through the thigh. But what I want to stress is Flaubert's description of the limb before this tragic performance. 'On that equine foot, which was indeed as broad as a horse's hoof, with horny skin, hard tendons, great thick toes and black toenails like the nails of a horseshoe – on that foot [Hippolyte] galloped about like a stag from morn to night. . . . He seemed actually stronger on that leg than on the other. With long service it had developed as it were moral qualities of energy and endurance, and on it he preferred to shore his weight when he had heavy work to do.' * Comment is needless.

The Galahad Syndrome

This is an interesting and well-known set-up between a male surgeon and a female patient, in which a series of surgical procedures is carried out, all unsuccessful and leading to progressive disability. It is pre-eminently an orthopaedic exercise, but it does also occur in abdominal and neurological surgery, and in the end one's heart sinks every time this professional victim – for that is what she is – is wheeled, beaming but complaining, into the clinic by her appendage of a husband.

What is really happening is a game in which the woman says: 'I bet you can't do a big operation on me and cure me !', and the surgeon is unwise enough to take the bet. The patient's quite real sufferings are accompanied by important secondary gains; she becomes the permanent invalid with a docile trapped attendant. (I often think that if their husbands ran away, some of these women would recover out of sheer pique.) But, at another level, this is also a seduction. There must be a strong sexual component because it so rarely happens *vis-à-vis* male patients. But it is a chivalrous sexuality on behalf of a poor, fluttering, defenceless creature (who is really as hard as nails), hence the name of the syndrome. I suppose the scalpel is one way of making love to a woman whose message is: 'Do with me what you will, as long as you don't expect me to get better !'

If the lady plays the game the hard way, very severe crippling and mutilation may result. There is one very well-known, but fortunately very rare type of malignant masochistic hysteric, the progressive amputee, who manages to have a limb removed at successively higher levels by producing a clinical picture of pain, swelling, numbness and paralysis. Sometimes the patients achieve this by secretly tying a ligature or elastic band round the part; but it is difficult to catch them at it.

For the sake of completeness it may be added that, although male patients do not behave like this (perhaps they would if they had women surgeons !), they do sometimes exhibit what has been called the Munchausen syndrome, in which a man, terribly scarred on the

* Gustave Flaubert, *Madame Bovary,* transl. Alan Russell. Penguin Books, 1950.

abdomen, appears at one hospital after another in apparent extremis, and tells a farrago of lies with the object of securing a stay in hospital, even if it means another unnecessary operation. Unmasked, he immediately loses his symptoms and discharges himself. Hospitals keep a black book of these individuals and exchange information about them : 'So-and-so is heading your way!' It is really a tramp's behaviour with a masochistic flavour, and the operation is the fee paid for admission to the workhouse.

Hubris

Last on our list is the sin of spiritual pride. In surgery this leads to ignoring natural processes and substituting artificial methods of cure. This is all very well so long as we remain aware of exactly what it is we have set aside. Our new weapons – transfusion, antibiotics, steroid hormones, nuclear medicine – supplant and suppress the natural responses of reaction and repair. But, as Horace wrote, 'Nature returns even if you expel her with a pitchfork', and if our modern measures fail, then we are flung back to the rule of a natural law we may no longer be able to understand, and thus discipline. It is really a matter of recognizing, as the Greeks did, that in the end necessity is the master of all men. As Thomas paradoxically put it, 'Nature can be subdued only by understanding, that is by obeying it.'

Even after having examined the various manifestations of the *furor therapeuticus,* however, the case against surgical interference cannot be summed up simply as a case against poor judgment and faulty technique. It cannot be argued that the bad results of surgery are no more that the results of bad surgery, and that careful selection and management can eliminate these errors. My argument goes far beyond this, into a different sphere: the sphere of irreducible error. By this I mean that, however careful the judgment, however meticulous the technique, there is a quite inevitable incidence of morbidity and mortality attached to operations and anaesthetics. Complications occur with a frequency which could quite probably be estimated actuarially, and all our care can only reduce these dangers to a minimum. The curve of surgical progress is what the mathematicians call an asymptotic one: it can only approach, but never reach, the base-line. We shall have disasters with us as long as there are surgeons and patients; and their existence is the permanent argument which the elective operator must defeat with more powerful counter-argument if he is to justify his activities. (I do not speak of the occasions when his hand is forced by the overriding urgencies of injury or or disease.)

I illustrate this with the case of a young man who had suffered a broken ankle and was left with increasing pain and stiffness. The surgeon (not myself this time) warned him that osteoarthritis was inevitable and advised an operation to render the joint stiff but painless. The patient agreed, the operation was done, the wound became infected, and he ended up with a below-knee amputation which took months to heal. This operation, which was performed on the most reasonable grounds and by a first-class surgeon, falls into my category of irreducible error. In prospect, the choice given the patient by the surgeon lay between an irritable joint, to which he could adjust his life and work, and a firm, stable ankle fit for any task. In retrospect, the Fates had given him quite a different choice: between staying as he was, and having an amputation – an irremediable tragedy. I quote this case to show the risks implicit in any surgical decision and to stress that we are not, and can never be, wholly in charge of the consequences flowing from such a decision.

To state the matter simply: surgery is not mathematics. It is never possible to prove regularly, in advance, that the outcome of an operation will be what is was intended to be. And if this is true of established procedures, how much more true must it be of newly-devised techniques. When a really novel procedure is introduced, one that may offer great hope of solving some stubborn problem, it is an unfortunate but unavoidable fact that the only way to find out if it is any good is to try it and see. And once we have tried it, it is too late to undo any bad results. For example, when operation for lumbar disc prolapse was introduced on a large scale at the end of the war, it was known to be capable of brilliant successes. (It still is.) All the old myths about sciatica were swept away and replaced by an identifiable and surgically accessible lesion. Logic and technique promised relief from this affliction; and in the excitement it was forgotten that no attack of sciatica lasts for ever, and that recovery is the rule if one waits long enough. Of course one has to know *how* to wait. In the event, history records many first-class results; but it also records something that was not predicted – the dire results of interference with the lumbar nerve-roots, which could lead to serious and even permanent invalidism.

Some patients were operated on several times in attempts to relieve symptoms, each intervention provoking further adhesions. In final attempts to gain relief, operations to fix the spine were then performed, using bone-grafts, each with its own fresh hazards. Today operation for sciatica is being done far less often; and, in some centres, more time is actually spent on exploring old failures, failures that may be absolutely intractable. Looking back and trying to strike some sort of balance, it is clear that much harm, as well as a great deal of good has been done, and as usual with the best of intentions. My point is that the scientific approach, when it elucidates the cause of a disease, also implies the attempt to remove that cause; and new hazards are thereby introduced which can only be estimated in retrospect. And I see no way of avoiding this dilemma. It is inherent in surgery (and much else besides!). In surgery's triumphal car all the seats face backwards. We find it difficult to see exactly where we are going, but we have only too excellent a view of where we have been. Perhaps the retrospectoscope is the best instrument we have!

Another example is the plastic replacement of the head of the femur in cases of fracture or osteoarthritis, introduced by French surgeons in the 'fifties. It was a bold and brilliant conception. What could be more rational than to remove a damaged femoral head and substitute a smooth inert sphere? The early results were magnificent and thousands of such operations were soon performed all over the globe. But the years passed, the plastic began to yield and crack, the prostheses slipped, the failures mounted until more time was being spent in removing these devices than in inserting them, and the operation was finally abandoned leaving its wrecks behind to be salvaged as best may be. Science has since marched on to newer and better prostheses in rare and expensive metals. Again, this cycle was inevitable. Perhaps some preliminary basic research in physics and in experimental animal surgery might have helped; it is possible to have the right idea when the suitable technology is not yet available. But, in sum, the episode was unavoidable.

It is right to do these new operations carefully and thoughtfully, but we must recognize that there may be errors, and that these will become apparent only later. With so many new techniques, one difficulty results from the time-lag involved in developing and trying out a new method, publishing the early good results, and then admitting any late unsatisfactory features. Unfortunately this salutary last stage is too often omitted, and this means that other surgeons repeat the entire process, from initial enthusiasm to final disillusion. On more than one occasion I have taken great care and trouble to perfect a technique introduced by some European or American colleague, only to be told when I eventually met him in person: 'Oh, I gave that up years ago, the results were so bad!' Of course, it is difficult for any surgeon to evaluate his own work; ideally, follow-up studies should be made by an independent observer. However, surgeons are not always noted for their reserve in commenting on each other's performance, and the situation has its delicacies.

I have made out this case against surgical interference, well aware of all that can be said – and rightly said – on the other side; but in the belief that, even in the present state of surgery, something may be gained by restating the arguments for conservatism.

When we have to act, we can only do so as seems best under the circumstances: in humility, after calculating the risks and taking them when necessary – all with due regard for the dignity of the patient as a person and our own as therapists.

For how we should *not* act, I refer you again to D. H. Lawrence, in a little poem entitled 'The Scientific Doctor':

> When I went to the scientific doctor
> I realised what a lust there was in him to wreak
>   his so-called science on me
> And reduce me to the level of a thing.
> So I said: Good-morning! and left him.

*

> Pains known not to be mortal – toothache or gout – who reckons them in the catalogue of diseases?
>
> MONTAIGNE

The basic problem of increasingly sophisticated medical care in highly industrialized communities is the spread of the idea that there is, or should be, a cure for everything, from life-threatening disorders down to the minor inconveniences of daily life: inconveniences which, in a previous epoch, would never have been rated as requiring medical attention at all.

It is a problem of escalation, with every successive medical court of appeal automatically entailing increasing costs, complexity of treatment and greater hazards. It is also a problem of the denial to the citizen – a denial he is only too willing to suffer – of his right and responsibility to bear pain, in private and with dignity: to suffer and die on his own account. Yet this has always been the human condition; we do suffer and die alone. But the current ethos is that someone ought to take this burden off our shoulders, as if Hygeia were an Alcestis for Everyman; that death itself is an unwarranted imposition, an intrusive vulgarian. In the welfare state, sickness is seen as a social solecism, to be absolved by act of Parliament. Hence there has been created a whole apparatus, a hierarchical system of medicine, a self-maintaining and expanding structure with an *investment* in disease – with which it is symbiotic – and with an unprecedented power of actually *creating* disease.

Then there is the screening of entire communities for the earliest signs of various diseases – diabetes, hypertension, heart-disease, cancer – on the assumption that early detection will allow their prevention or cure, an assumption that has yet to be borne out by the facts. There is also individual screening, as of the middle-aged executive: a subjection to batteries of tests, all of which is very generative of hypochondria, of fearful self-scrutiny ('Have you examined your breasts today?') and perhaps of very little else.

I have little time or patience for all this. My maxim is: leave well alone. Where there are no symptoms, do not enquire within. I believe that the major health advances have come from progress in public hygiene, and that the individual is to be saved from degenerative disease by individual hygiene inculcated in the earliest years – sane habits of eating and exercise and relaxation, the avoidance of tobacco and alcohol. (How easy it is to say that, when for millions life would be intolerable without these anodynes!)

Let us take a simple example of medical escalation, that of low back pain and sciatica. For many centuries this was regarded as what it is, a natural affection of the human body, to be borne stoically till it got better – which it nearly always does – and not a matter for medical care at all. ('But pray, Sir, what was your father doing all December, January and February?' 'Why, Madam – he was all that time afflicted with a Sciatica.' *Tristram Shandy*.) The first escalation came from the spread of the idea, at the turn of the century, that every pain should be reported to a general practitioner and that the cost of the consulta- tion should be borne by the State, a trend superficially desirable and progressive. Pain is pain, and the doctors had the key of the medicine chest. The main objection to this is that the more we regard ourselves as entitled to immediate relief, the less tolerant we become of any pain at all. This is one reason why our forbears were perfectly well able to endure operations without anaesthesia – there was no alternative. One thinks of Josiah Wedgwood in the eighteenth century, asking the surgeons to amputate a chronically swollen leg because it was a nuisance. The hope of something better always impairs our powers of sustaining the actual.

This escalation entails much expenditure and organization by the State. The drugs may be expensive and the doctor, by supplying the certificate, sets the seal on the patient's invalidity. In this sense he *creates* incapacity, for the patient feels he must be ill to merit such attention. Of course, some patients abuse the relationship and are glad to stay at home, cushioned by sickness benefit. One is repeatedly struck by the difference in recovery rates between the ordinary, em- ployed patient, and the self-employed or private one. The latter is more independent; he is losing by being ill; financial interest rein- forces the natural urge to return to activity. The former, especially if cossetted in hospital, is often only too willing to remain dependent. I have had private patients back in the office a week after a disc opera- tion; most others take at least a month. But, to be fair, there is a reverse side to this: the reparative urge may make a doctor keep on a patient longer than necessary, as if to discharge him were to terminate a relationship that had become of value to both parties. Yet the patient may not always welcome this situation, may even find it irk- some. Between this danger and that of the exploitation of the doctor by the patient, one must steer a middle course.

The second, and fateful, stage of escalation is when the doctor refers our sciatic sufferer to an orthopaedic specialist at a hospital. Here again we have what appears to be a socially useful measure. But the nature of the disorder will not have changed; only the techniques applied will rise to new levels of complexity, and the costs and risks of treatment will be correspondingly increased. Merely to be seen in hospital makes the patient fearful. In order that he shall be seen at all, an expensive network of clinics, clerks and consultants has to exist. An X-ray will almost certainly be expected. This calls for another expensive department, exposes the patient and his germ-cells to the hazards of radiation, and may not be necessary at all – for a specialist diploma is no guarantee of common sense.

Here the consultant is trapped between what he knows about the natural history of lumbago – that the vast majority of cases are transient and harmless – and what is expected of him by the patient and the State. He knows that an X-ray is rarely necessary at the first visit except when certain clinical features make it desirable to exclude inflammatory or malignant spinal disorders: that there will be time enough for an X-ray if symptoms persist. Also, that it is possible to take an X-ray *too early* in the evolution of a serious condition, before its characteristic signs have developed, thus obscuring the diagnosis. Yet, though common sense often contra-indicates an X-ray, the patient may feel himself denied or deprived. We all know how delightfully therapeutic it is to be transfixed by the magic rays. The consultant may feel happier for having done what was expected of him, especially as not having an X-ray – even an unnecessary one – may expose him to charges of negligence. So he will tend to play safe and the gain will have been nil. And yet all this will be taken as part and proof of a progressive system of national health care.

A further danger is that the X-ray may show *something*. This is a risk that is rather difficult to convey to the layman, who may feel that, if anything untoward is shown, this must be to the good. But the X-ray film is not the flesh-and-blood patient; it is only an appearance and any abnormality of profile it may reveal may be merely incidental. The film of our sufferer may show, for instance, that one vertebra has slipped forward on another. This is not uncommon, it is not usually progressive, and most cases need no treatment. It is an incidental finding; but it *is* an orthopaedic abnormality and it tends to excite vigorous reflex therapeutic activity in some surgeons, especially if they are young, energetic, recently appointed, bored, or merely deficient in common sense and clinical experience. For there is an operation for this condition, a major procedure designed to fix the affected segment of the spine by bone-grafting. Necessary or not, this entails months of hospitalization, invalidism and loss of production. It is the final escalation, as would also be an operation to remove a prolapsed disc. I have discussed this elsewhere. I recall treating conservatively a German visitor who boasted: '*Our* orthopaedic surgeons know how to *operate* on discs!' To which I could only reply: 'Yes, and here we have learned how *not* to operate!'

If our sufferer is lucky enough to remain an outpatient, he may be given various forms of treatment: physiotherapy, which postulates the existence of yet another department with its costly staff and equipment, but which offers little more than does rest in bed; spinal injections, calling for a disposable syringe service and expensive drugs; or manipulation, which often requires anaesthesia and its hazards. If, on the other hand, he is admitted to hospital, costs really begin to rise when we consider the relevant quota of beds, nursing, ancillary services and hotel charges borne by the State. And all the time he is in hospital he is exposed to therapeutic teams whose function is to treat, and to be seen to be treating, with all the paraphernalia available. Of operation and its perils I have already spoken.

This vast apparatus can clearly generate disease and disability if mishandled; and it is bound to be mishandled from time to time because doctors, and especially surgeons, have the urge or are urged, to do something. It requires great restraint for the clinician to wait and see, rather than to look and see. In the field of abdominal disorder, especially, he will increasingly favour the latter course. And yet, when one looks round a hospital ward it is inescapable that a sizeable proportion of the patients are suffering from the results of previous treatment or investigation, rather than from any original disease itself.

9

In the foregoing essays, which were written some time ago, I deliberately overstated the case against sophisticated medicine because it has rarely been even stated; or not until recently. So it was exciting much later to come across Ivan Illich and his book Medical Nemesis, *and to find that our views frequently coincided. Many of my readers may already know this book.* I strongly advise those who do not, to study it, for Illich's arguments are relevant, urgent and important. I am going to summarize them now at considerable length, sticking closely to his own language, using quotation marks where material has been directly transposed and square brackets for my own occasional interpolations.*

The medical establishment has become a major threat to health. The damage it does outweighs the benefits, for it supersedes the power of the individual to heal himself and shape his environment; it aims to convince people that it is *they* who are sick, and not society.

The damage done by medicine is *clinical* when it directly causes pain, illness and death; *social* when it underpins an industrial set-up that generates ill-health; and *structural,* when it undermines individual responsibility in growing, ageing, dying and answering the challenge of disease. Institutional medicine has created a new kind of suffering: 'an anaesthetised, impotent and solitary survival in a world turned into a hospital ward'.

Illich likens modern medicine to an epidemic. The virtual disappearance of the killing disorders from the West is not to be equated with medical care; tuberculosis, cholera, typhoid and other fevers declined *before* there was any specific medical treatment, and even before improved hygiene and housing: it was due to increased resistance resulting from better nutrition. Where malnutrition persists in poor countries, infection is still far more severe [as I found with bone infections in Iran]. In the West, the infectious and dietary diseases of

---

* Ivan Illich, *Medical Nemesis*. Calder & Boyars, 1975.

146

the nineteenth century, with their high infantile mortality, have been replaced by the stress disorders of later life, such as coronary disease, hypertension and mental illness; but medicine did not eliminate the former, nor did it create the increased life-span which gave time for the new diseases to develop.

It is environment that primarily determines the health of populations. True, some modern techniques to do with water supplies and sewage and vaccination have shifted mortality from children to adults; but there is no real evidence that medical services are responsible for the striking changes in the pattern of disease. That certain diseases have become rare where doctors are many is only because doctors congregate where conditions are good and patients can pay. [And, *per contra,* though Illich does not say this, the high disease rate in Asiatic villages probably only correlates with the absence of doctors in the sense that the latter prefer not to work there.]

Admittedly, there are a few diseases where specific treatment or prevention are effective, such as venereal infection, malaria, typhoid and poliomyelitis; but for many disorders the effectiveness of treatment is questionable. Thus it is doubtful whether any form of treatment improves survival in breast and other cancers, however early detected. [It is often argued – and persuasively to the lay mind – that the earlier treatment is carried out in malignant disease, the better the prospects of cure, being assessed in years of survival rather than in absolute terms. But a moment's thought shows that this is not necessarily the case. A patient with an early cancer will live longer than one with a late growth, and if treatment is applied at an early stage it will be credited with a longer survival, although this merely reflects the natural history of the disease.]

Illich stresses *iatrogenic disease* – disease created by the doctor during treatment. Drugs may have unwanted side-effects, may be addictive or mutagenic. Antibiotics may encourage the growth of super-organisms. Surgery is often unnecessary [and may be predicated by the ratio of surgeons to patients and the availability of fees.] Disabling 'non-diseases' may be created. In the United States accidents are the major cause of death in children, and most of these occur in hospital. In university hospitals one in five of admitted patients develops an iatrogenic disorder.

Socially, medicine is dysgenic in that it preserves mental and physical degenerates, the permanently unfit individual. It paralyses healthy responses to suffering and replaces them with a form of sub-lethal medical engineering. This is the medical nemesis, and it can be reversed only by recognition and recovery of the right to mutual self-care by the laity.

Although the British National Health Service was expected to reduce sickness rates, these have risen; the definition of sickness and the scope of medicine have expanded as individual tolerance and responsibility for disability and disease have declined. In the West, belief in unlimited 'progress' has been taken to include progress in medical engineering, despite the demonstrable fact that suffering and costs increase with treatment.

More and more money is spent on medical care, and not only in the richer countries. (Nevertheless 'tight-fisted misallocations and a stern commitment to equality' have saved Britain from much of America's 'prestigious gadgetry'.) And modern equipment costs more, and breaks down more often, in the less developed countries [though, as in Iran, such equipment and such hospitals may be developed for prestige purposes in the cities while rural areas have virtually no health services at all.]

Doctors, like motor-cars, are noxious because they both actively cause harm and encourage passive consumer dependence. Drug abuse increases, not in the sense of narcotic dependence but in over con-sumption of powerful medicaments – antibiotics, tranquillizers and anti-depressants – even where doctors are scarce. The *life-span* becomes medicalized. The natural ages and stages of life are all seen as periods requiring specific therapies and therapists. Yet most diseases are self-limiting, and medicine can only protract most of the disorders of old age to create a geriatric problem group. Other age-groups – infants, adolescents, pregnant and menopausal women – are similarly labelled as special forms of medical clientele.

Preventive health – screening, the check-up – has become a status symbol. People have become patients without being ill. There are well-person clinics for infants, children and the middle-aged – soph-isticated assembly-line testing. Yet these procedures have no impact on life expectancy, create hypochondria, are often dangerous and sometimes lethal, and those tested – who had thought themselves well – risk being submitted to unnecessary, unpleasant and expensive treatments. Such screening treats people as machines requiring regu-lar servicing.

Intensive care creates new problems: the selected few with kidney failure, whose lives are uncomfortably prolonged by renal dialysis; intensive hospital care for heart-attack patients [who, as has been shown, do better at home], the preservation of living bodies with dead brains. There is a deep-seated need for miracle cures, such as heart-transplants, in the heroic medical struggle against death, a fear of unmedicalized death without expert supervision. All these modern techniques produce an aura of magic and ritual; and yet therapy is increasingly centred on death rather than life. The modern doctor is the priest, magician and agent of the political establishment, and some of his ritual mutilations, such as tonsillectomy in children, are barbarous and unnecessary.

The sick citizen is cast as a deviant to be exempted from social obligations, incapable of self-repair without assistance from doctors who are also bureaucrats. They legitimize despair and disinclination for work with a sickness label, and this certification becomes a device for social control of the sick. All this is a by-product of our over-industrialized society. Until the late nineteenth century most treatment was provided by the family or the local community; industrialization has created a spiritual poverty which thwarts the capacity of the individual to cope with the challenge of sickness by adapting his body or his environment. Yet the main concern of medicine remains sick individuals rather than the health of populations.

The basic problem is independent of financial gain by the doctors, for it is there whether they practise privately or as civil servants. It arises from medical *monopoly* as such, and will not necessarily be solved by turning independent practitioners into salaried state servants; indeed it might become worse as medicine becomes more legitimized and 'altruistic'. As long as doctors decide what constitutes good service, medical facilities can never be costed. And as medical specialities proliferate, their position is at the apex of a hierarchy whose lower levels are various grades of ancillary workers, a sub-proletariat of [largely foreign] nurses and hospital staff.

'Medical science' is now a quasi-ecclesiastical monopoly which makes the historically novel assumption that all ills are to be treated, whatever the outcome, an arrogant form of therapeutic mania. But human beings are unique in their awareness of frailty and inevitable death, and their cultures aim to perfect their ability to deal with these threats. There is no 'norm' for physical health, only different local sets of rules for meeting pain, disability and death. Yet these age-old human experiences are transformed into mere accidents requiring treatment, the antithesis of traditional cultures which equipped man to bear pain, tolerate sickness and accept death. Natural healing, patience, fortitude and compassion give way to passive medical manipulation. Pain, suffering and death are no longer experiences to be interpreted – meaningful sources of courage, self-control and resignation – but problems to be eliminated. Pain has become a political evil. Suffering is no longer a positive and productive art, but an irrelevance to be technically abolished.

Our experience of physical pain is, in fact, largely determined by social and cultural settings and expectations. The *loneliness* of pain excites a peculiar compassion; and the way in which pain is experienced depends on the personality of the sufferer, and this is shaped by society. But it is now the medical profession that judges which pains are authentic, and society is trained to value anaesthesia [to the extent that leucotomized patients have been surgically tamed by brain operations to experience pain as mild discomfort].

In the western world, until well on in the seventeenth century, pain was an essential component of life in this vale of tears, the bitter taste of reality in an inevitably defective universe. Only later was it re-categorized as a biological early warning system whose passive victims were to be helped from a drug cabinet to which the doctors held the key. And the other side of the picture is that, in an anaesthetized society, stronger and stronger stimuli – drugs, sex, violence – are required to persuade people that they are alive and that their life is meaningful. Instead of suffering with dignity, the drugged become 'unfeeling spectators of their own decaying selves.' [If it is true that I suffer, therefore I am; what happens when I do not suffer?]

By the mid-nineteenth century the doctor had become a culture-hero, and the ordinary ailments of life had been catalogued as specific diseases in a quasi-botanical system, entities to be studied and manipulated. Medical interest shifted from the sick to sickness, and persons became cases. The hospital, originally a pesthouse, became a repair-shop; society became a clinic. Yet 'disease' is largely a socially created reality; and this is most evident in the context of mental illness, for the psychiatrist operates only within socially or politically determined co-ordinates.

Our over-industrialized society *creates* disease, in the sense that people do not fit into it; and their inability to do so is diagnosed as a health defect, while the social institutions themselves are exonerated. Where the patient once saw in the doctor's eyes, the reflection of his own anguish, he now meets the gaze of an accountant. The doctor's very language is a mystification. Yet most measures that do more good than harm are cheap and can be applied by members of the family or by instructed laymen. In other words, medicine needs to be 'deprofessionalized'. A good example of deprofessionalization is pregnancy testing and abortion by vacuum extraction – safe, simple and cheap. Deprofessionalization does not deny the importance of competent specialists. It does imply a bias against the mystification of the public by legally approved and self-accredited healers who control the allocation of funds, against the lavish use of resources for a few, against state provision of magic technical devices and dependence on institutions rather than persons.

Death. The idea of 'natural' death in old age and in good health under medical supervision is a recent one. People were once taught to die with dignity, to be ready; at one time it was blasphemous for doctors even to think of prolonging life. Nowadays death, if still inevitable, must be *timely*; and it is for the doctor to say when the clock must strike. Inevitable death has been replaced by a host of 'accidental' killer diseases. [Death, as Freud implies, has come to be regarded as an accident, almost an outrage, as letting the side down, as *undeserved*, as punishment, or else as an heroic undertaking.] Death has become a clinical event and death without medication has become almost criminal. The doctor interposes himself between humanity and death; it is he, rather than the patient, who struggles against it. [The modern corollary is that death is somebody's *fault*, due to a class enemy or social deprivation or a negligent doctor.] And these capitalist expectations have been adopted by the trades unions.

Socially, hospitalized death is the goal of economic development, and people become simply unable to die with any realistic attitude towards death. The arrival of social security means that death must not take place except as specified by the medical umpire. 'Death has become the point at which the living organism refuses any further input of treatment . . . it is the ultimate form of consumer resistance.' Society, through the doctor, decides when, and after what indignities, the sick man shall die.

What to do? The Promethean rebel against the human condition falls prey to Nemesis, the penalty for *hubris*. Our modern Nemesis is the backlash of industrial progress, and an engineered harassment is now the main source of pain, suffering and death. In this context, modern medicine is the priesthood of Tantalus, offering unlimited improvement in human health. It is also a maintenance system on behalf of the industrial system and a systematized delusion about the true nature and meaning of life. Together with society's other institutions, the medical industry needs to be disestablished.

The answer is not to be found in better social engineering or new ecological dogma. We have to recognize that there are limits to human action, for, deprived of the limits once laid down by the Gods, we now behave as if there were no restraints on human ingenuity. In a framework deprived of its sacred character we need a new ethical imperative: 'Act so that the effect of your action is compatible with the permanence of genuine human life.' For example: 'Do not raise radiation levels unless you know that this action will not be visited on your grandchild.'

Can we attain this ethic in a secular society? Can we realize that there are things we are able to do, yet which ought not to be done? What we need is to reverse industrial expansion, to recognize how much the environment can tolerate, to adjust organization to the autonomous pursuit of individual and equitable aims. In medicine this means that people will limit therapy because they want to retain their own power to heal. Better health must come from increasing competence in self-care, and medical technology should be proscribed until those devices and procedures that can be handled by laymen become truly available to them. People made ill by their life and work should not be cast in the roles of patients, but allowed to opt for a less destructive way of life. People should be left to define their own health, and healers should be evaluated by the community rather than by their own professional guilds.

Health denotes the ability to adapt to natural changes within the individual and in the environment. 'It includes anguish, and the inner resources to live with it.' For human beings health is a *task* (it is not the natural physiology of the beasts), and success in this task requires self-awareness and self-discipline, the regulation of action, appetite and sex in responsible patterns within the dynamic stability of a cul-

ture. The ability to cope with illness can be enhanced, but never replaced, by medical intervention; the best conditions for health are
those in which such intervention is reduced to a minimum.

'Experience of pain, sickness and death is an integral part of life,
coping with them independently a fundamental of health. . . .
Healthy people are those who live in healthy homes on a healthy diet
. . . sustained by a culture which enhances the conscious acceptance
of limits to population, of ageing . . . and ever-imminent death.
Healthy people need no bureaucratic interference to mate, give birth,
share the human condition and die. . . . The true miracle of modern
medicine . . . consists not only of making individuals but whole populations survive on inhumanly low levels of personal health.'

What we actually have is 'an unhealthy society that depends on unhealthy people whose survival, discipline and functioning are assured
through delivery of the necessary therapeutic services. . . . Either the
natural boundaries of human endeavour are estimated, recognised
and translated into politically determined limits, or the alternative to
extinction is accepted as compulsory survival in a planned and engineered hell.'

A parable in support of Illich.

A little old lady, chirpy as a sparrow, glowing with health, presents
herself in the clinic with a lump in one arm. I do not know what it is;
there are several things it may be. Intuition suggests a chest X-ray,
though I know, as I fill in the request, that this may be a bit too clever,
that it may be better not to know. However, the reflexes have been
excited and the rest is inexorable. The lungs are full of secondaries,
rounded and opaque as cannon-balls. Removing the swelling in the
arm is simple; examination shows it to be a malignant tumour of
muscle. We are now left with an old lady who has no chest symptoms
whatever and no idea of her true condition. Common sense would
say nothing and send her home with a pat on the back. But 'scientific'
medicine wins the day; her lungs are irradiated and she is given large
doses of cytotoxic drugs. So her last few weeks are – in a thoroughly
orthodox way – made miserable with distressing treatments; and,
what is worse, like so many cancer patients, at no time does she ask
point-blank what it is all in aid of. If she had not been so treated, she
would have remained well until shortly before the end, and then died
fairly rapidly and painlessly. I am not sure that we have even pro-

longed her life. Quite often in surgery, as here, to do the right thing is to do the wrong thing. To satisfy our therapeutic urge, to avoid charges of negligence, we are guilty of officious and over-zealous interference which may be even more damaging.

Montaigne seems to have anticipated Illich. 'Whoever would take away the knowledge and sense of evil would, at the same time, eradicate the sense of pleasure and, in short, annihilate man himself.' Or again, 'We are not so sensible of the most perfect health as we are of the least sickness.' Illich seems to see the doctor's attitude to disease as something akin to Swift's portrayal of the clergy's attitude to the Devil: 'They believe in him, they have an *Interest* in him, and therefore they are the greatest supports of his kingdom.'

To some extent Illich is a Utopian, and uses medicine as a stalking horse to his real target, which is the industrialized state (to deal with which would probably automatically improve the medical situation). Modern technology has certainly brought enormous disadvantages but it has also brought enormous benefits; and for societies which have enjoyed these for generations, any attempt to put the machine into reverse must be seen and felt as an intolerable deprivation. Moreover, quite apart from the benefits it is intended to bring, technology is increasingly valuable and pleasurable for its own sake. We cannot run away from technology at this time of day, and it may be that the only answer to industrialization is not to retreat but to go forward and grow through the situation. It is essential not to throw away the baby with the bathwater. But most of us probably agree that it is unreasonable and damaging to expect the Third World to follow in our footsteps; though its inhabitants, seeing only the glittering superficial aspect of our industrial goodies, may suspect us of a dog-in-the-manger attitude here.

The money spent on technological solutions to individual diseases – and diseases of individuals – in industrial societies vastly exceeds that spent on dealing with epidemics and malnutrition, yet it produces little improvement in general well-being. Yet, at the same time, 'progress' creates an insatiable demand for medical treatment. (I agree with Baudelaire that universal progress – or universal ruin, they are the same – can only be marked by *l'avilissement des coeurs*; that there can be no true, i.e. moral, progress except in the individual and through the individual.) The major part of our medical resources is devoted to a hospital-oriented system of care with an emphasis on drugs and operative treatment. Whether the overall health of the population has been improved thereby is very doubtful. But there is no conceivable limit to technical advance. The whole of the money now spent on the National Health Service could easily be spent on a national heart or kidney or rheumatic service. And, since physical and financial resources are limited even in the wealthiest states, 'progress' is self-destructive and noxious to basic health requirements, which are: preventive measures for the common disorders, improved nutrition, housing and sanitation, and – more debatably – an expansion of primary medical care by general practitioners and by paramedical auxiliaries, trained to recognize and treat common problems at an early stage within the setting of the local community.

All very well, but can we apply Illich's views everywhere? I think not. In Asia and Africa there exist serious prevalent endemic disorders, problems of communicable disease and malnutrition such as malaria and hook worm and protein insufficiency, which *cannot* be cured within the local framework and *must* be dealt with by importing new technology from outside. In some cases half of all children born die; hence large families, to ensure a sufficiency of survivors and to provide for the parents in their old age. We cannot condemn the Third World to permanent poverty and disease because we want to preserve an idyllic innocence. There never really was a noble savage from the hygienic point of view. The benefits of modern medicine are indisputable, even if they are not accompanied by corresponding advances in the public health; it cannot be helped if the initial effect of disease control is a rise in population. Unfortunately the politicians in the underdeveloped countries – and not only in these – have been encouraged to believe that all that needs to be done to improve health is to spend a lot of money on new hospitals and medical schools (which produce technicians, not humanists). This is not so. The benefits are only minor and are not reflected in vital statistics; for food, housing and preventive hygiene are what count.

On the other hand, in Western countries (why do we continue to say Western when we really mean Northern?) it is certainly wasteful and injurious dysgenically to preserve the lives of those whose lethal genes are transmitted to their offspring; to save surgically children with grave congenital deformities; to screen, detect and treat with expensive drugs cases of symptomless hypertension and diabetes; to embark on questionable programmes of organ transplantation. Many of the things made possible by modern medical techniques are of the same order of achievement – and of general usefulness – as putting a man on the moon. To repeat, because a thing *can* be done, it does not follow that it *should* be done.

The retreat from technology is not exactly a new call. To some extent Illich seems biased by his experience of high-pressure North American medicine and the attempts to misapply it to Central and Southern America. He seems unacquainted with the common sense of the good British general practitioner. The medical profession itself has never lacked for self-criticism, and many of us have already said some of the things Illich is now saying. The basic question is whether cultural evolution can be put into reverse. This is Illich's solution; but is it possible?

As a surgeon, I feel that surgery is both particularly vulnerable and particularly immune to his criticisms. We *have* built up an empire of elaborate technical procedures, fascinating in themselves and too often an end in themselves; a repair system which does not wait or want to consider why the mechanism went wrong in the first place and which, like many automobile repair-shops, sometimes seems to cure the original fault at the expense of creating new ones. And which is better: to invest enormous sums and technique and energy in replacing worn-out coronary arteries or removing cancerous lungs with highly dubious benefits, or to teach people so to live that their hearts are kept healthy by exercise and their lungs unpoisoned by cigarette smoke? Some 30,000 men in the prime of life die annually in this country from lung cancer, not to speak of the morbidity and mortality due to heart-disease and bronchitis, and the women are beginning to catch up. I sometimes think that surgeons should fold their hands and say to the politicians: 'We're tired of this. It's unnecessary. It's your turn now to stop this nonsense.' A society which had no rubbish collection service would soon learn to dispose of it in other ways, or not to generate it. Why should we continue to operate a medical and psychiatric service for dealing with garbage which need not have been generated in the first place? We do not need industrial hygienists to tell miners that their work is literally sickening, or psychiatrists to tell the mothers of young children that their place is in the home.

But do individual pain and suffering never rightly require medical aid? The obverse of the coin is the saving of the individual life, the midnight appendicectomy, the repair of a ruptured aneurism. I don't think any layman, however well-informed, is going to be able to replace the highly-trained surgeon here. The urge to save the individual life is far older than industrialization.

Although I share Illich's adverse criticism of the medical establishment to a very large extent, he seems to me to be an excellent diagnostician but a doubtful therapist. His proposals for reform are sadly lacking in definition and sometimes seem to approach the impracticality of D. H. Lawrence's ideas on the reform of industrial society: that the miners, for instance, instead of mining, should do Morris dances in the streets in coloured tunics. But it is surely true that we must begin to recover our responsibility for our own health from the professionals. Illich's basic argument is surely right. It is the argument of Montaigne, with whom we began: 'Living is slavery if the liberty of dying be wanting. The ordinary method of cure is carried on at the expense of life.'

10

Thou has bound bones and veins in me,
fastened me flesh . . .

GERARD MANLEY HOPKINS

In everyday life we see ourselves and those we meet as no more than talking heads. Our bodies, concealed by clothes, are mere appendages which we feed and water, exercise and sexually indulge, as we might pet dogs. The body is not sung or celebrated – in art, athletics and sexual prowess – except in its superficies. Were we to see each other habitually naked, we should not mentally so distance ourselves from our animal kin.

But our internal organs are never praised. Their beauties are never discussed and we take no pride in their possession. We can enjoy the beauty of our own or another's breast, the line of a nose or the curve of a buttock. We do not equally admire the glossy red bulge of the liver, the glistening white convolutions of the brain, the elegant villi of the intestine. Our internal organs are hidden away, like poor relations, except when their clamorous demands for attention call for appeasement with drug or knife. But generally these messages from the interior do not reach consciousness except in the neurotic, in whom they reinforce, with their hell of hypochondria, the equally disturbing input from the environment. The result is a situation in which the sufferer, like Christian in the *Pilgrim's Progress*, looks this way and that as if he would run, yet stands still because he cannot tell which way to go.

For everyman and everyday, perhaps this is just as well. Ignorance is health. We do not function any the better for knowing about our internal milieu. We do not identify ourselves with our internal organs, or them with us; matters of sewage and internal traffic are beneath our concern. To know how our leg muscles work helps us not one whit to walk; and if we did know, and pondered on it, walking would

158

become an impossibility. We can safely leave most of our bodily functions to the automatic pilot; though sometimes, like Palinurus, he may fall asleep at the wheel.

But for the artist, pictorial or literary, the inner world is a legitimate object for portrayal; and it is surprising how rarely the opportunity has been taken, for, unlike the animals, we not only know that we are going to die, we also know that we are more than a surface. There is the Bible, which is very conscious of loins and bowels and bones; but even the Song of Solomon sticks to the exterior. There is Whitman's marvellous poem, *I Sing the Body Electric,* which I wish I could quote entire:

> Gentlemen, look on this wonder . . .
> In this head the all-baffling brain . . .
> Examine these limbs, red, black or white, they are
>   cunning in tendon and nerve . . .
> Within there runs blood,
> The same old blood! The same red-running blood!
> There swells and jets a heart, there all passions,
>   desires, reachings, aspirations,
> (Do you think they are not there because they are
>   not express'd in parlors and lecture-rooms?)

This same poem includes a wonderful anatomical catalogue which refers to: 'The lung-sponges, the stomach-sac, the bowels sweet and clean/The brain in its folds inside the skull-frame. . . . The thin red jellies within you or within me/The bones and the marrow in the bones/The exquisite realization of health/O I say these are not the parts and poems of the body only, but of the soul/O I say now these are the soul!'

But of course it is the skeleton that has most impressed the ordinary man, because it lasts so long after the body has corrupted: Housman's 'stedfast and enduring bone', the dry bones of Ezekiel. It was the man of bone within that became the emblem of mortality in the mediaeval Dance of Death. Still, most of us are content with ignorance and the surface appearances. Certainly, Swift thought it a mistake to enquire within: 'In most Corporeal Beings which have fallen under my Cognizance, the Outside hath been infinitely preferable to the In . . . Last Week I saw a Woman flay'd, and you will hardly believe how much it altered her Person for the worse!' And he goes on: 'Yesterday I ordered the Carcass of a Beau to be stript in my Presence; when we were all amazed to find so many unsuspected Faults under one Suit of Cloaths. Then I laid open his Brain, his Heart and his Spleen. But I plainly perceived at every Operation that the farther we proceeded, we found the Defects encrease upon us in Number and Bulk.' So, Swift argues, rather than Anatomy being the ultimate end of Physick, it is satisfaction with the outer aspect of things that provides the greatest felicity, for 'Happiness is the perpetual Possession of being well Deceived.'

So, in general, it has been left to the anatomist and the surgeon to note that we are 'fearfully and wonderfully made'; and to the microscopist to marvel at the beauty and intricacy of the cell, which could serve as a miracle of design to the instructed artist. This is one reason why I have so much enjoyed translating Monique Wittig's *Le Corps Lesbien,* which offers virtually nothing about lesbianism (incidentally, why is it that the word *lecteur* has none of the connotations of *voyeur*?) but a great deal about the internal organs as objects for contemplation or exploration.

And, of course, our bodies are swayed and stirred by our emotions. Sometimes this produces corresponding outward effects: we blush or squirm, are incontinent in an air-raid or when going over the top. Often the impulses to which we deny consciousness find an outlet by disturbing the function and even the structure of our organs to the point of psychosomatic disease. Think only of love: how we itch with desire when we have someone not so much under our skin but actually *dans la peau,* so that maybe certain syndromes of skin disease marked by redness and irritation are a devious expression of a desire we cannot bring ourselves to acknowledge; of how compassion, and love, can be felt literally in the bowels so that, parting from the loved object, one may experience violent physical abdominal disturbance; of how the nervous control of the heart may be stimulated by emotion until that organ beats faster or irregularly or suddenly ceases to function. To equate love with anxiety as a psychosomatic phenomenon, think only of Sappho's famous *Ode to Anactoria*:

> ... that sweet speech and lovely laughter, that indeed makes my heart flutter in my bosom. For when I see thee but a little, I have no utterance left, my tongue is broken down, and straightway a subtle fire has run under my skin; with my eyes I have no sight, my ears ring, sweat pours down and a trembling seizes my entire body; I am paler than grass, and seem in my madness little better than

dead . . .

Perhaps some such considerations operated in the minds of those who inflicted punishments in earlier days. Really to punish a traitor under Elizabeth I, he was first hanged, but not enough to lose consciousness; he was then cut down and made to witness his own evisceration; his genitalia were cut off and exhibited to him; only the removal of the heart brought surcease. That was real punishment, through and through. It was not just the talking head that was silenced; the whole man was exterminated.

The surgeon knows only too well that the stuff he works with is perishable. However inspired his efforts, nothing eventually remains. That is why every surgeon of feeling envies the creative artist, would like to reverse the achievement of Pygmalion. That is why Balzac says that surgeons are famous in the same way that actors are – only in their lifetime (or in that of their patients). Actors and surgeons, like musical virtuosi, are all heroes of the moment.

*

An old friend, Mrs A., died today. She was seventy-five. For a quarter of a century we had been engaged as partners in a slowly losing battle against a tumour – a sarcoma of low-grade malignancy – of the sciatic nerve in her left leg. It played cat-and-mouse with us. We would shell it out of the nerve-trunk; a few months – a year or two – later, it would reappear at another level. For a long time we were able to preserve nerve-function, but a day came when this was no longer possible and she developed foot-drop and had to wear an appliance. After fifteen years the tumour had grown so large at the knee that the limb could no longer be preserved and we did an amputation through the thigh. A year or two later large masses had developed where the nerve enters the pelvis, and as the tumour did not respond very well to irradiation or cytotoxic drugs, she underwent the operation of hindquarter amputation, a vast procedure – one of the most mutilating in surgery – in which the limb is removed from the trunk together with half the pelvis. Then, and then only, for the first time, the tumour lost its local character and reappeared under the skin half-way down the opposite thigh, as if mocking our endeavours, always one step ahead. By this time she was tired of operations and the situation was just kept under control for some years with X-ray treatment.

Then, a few days ago, she reappeared with a fracture of the right thigh-bone, eroded by the tumour. We were glad, as always, to see each other again, even though our meetings were always brought about by some such disaster; we were very fond of each other. She expressed utter confidence in my ability to deal with the situation and we fixed the fracture with a long nail passed down the marrow cavity of the bone, a simple procedure. But after that she gave us a terrible grey look, turned her face to the wall, and died; for no other reason than that she had had enough. I salute her spirit, which had enabled her to endure and lead an independent life for so long; and I am grateful that she gave me the opportunity to help her to do so.

By a strange coincidence, there was in the ward at the same time a young girl who had also undergone a hindquarter amputation. But in this case the entire limb with the side of the pelvis had been wrenched off in a motor accident. The police brought it along and one thought – but only briefly – of the possibility of reattaching it. (The Chinese, and almost only the Chinese, are very good at this, perhaps because of the incredibly patient and meticulous repair-work involved.) But to be at one moment a healthy young woman and then to awake from the accident and the anaesthetic to find that *that* had happened !

Mrs A.'s case reminded me of another sarcoma of the sciatic nerve in a young man, highly malignant this time, presenting as a lump the size of a golf-ball in the course of the nerve at the back of the thigh below the buttock. At the beginning we could only guess what this might be; and when it was exposed at operation it was difficult to say whether the tumour, which was expanding the nerve-trunk, was harmless and benign or aggressive and dangerous. If it was the latter, the only hope was to remove a long section of the nerve containing the tumour, with a good margin of healthy tissue on each side, and I did so. But the dilemma was a terrible one, for if I was wrong and the lesion proved microscopically to be benign, I would have produced total paralysis and loss of sensation below the knee to no purpose whatsoever. I passed a very unpleasant quarter of an hour – or rather two days – waiting for the pathologist's report. And, in the event, all turned out as well as it could do. Five years later he is fit and well and in active employment, and though he wears an appliance to control his foot, he has normal agility. The tumour has not recurred. But we must keep our fingers crossed.

I have to add – and with what pleasure! – that the partners of these two young people, to whom they were engaged, stood by them and married them. And this is the counterpart to the unpleasantnesses one sees so often in clinical life. There is no limit to the nobility, any more than there is to the wickedness, of human beings. *L'homme ne peut pas toujours mal faire.*

11

Tonight I find myself thinking of G.: physician, colleague over many years, the only friend I made in adult life, a man who changed my life utterly, jolting me out of my small suburban groove for ever.

He was the possessor of a singularly original mind, untainted with the least hint of reverence for established authority. Though vaguely aware of each other's existence for some years, we did not become closely acquainted until the brief preliminary report of a new and revolutionary treatment for rheumatoid arthritis in the *Lancet* by two Swedish workers brought us together for a clinical trial. It so happened that the very first patient we treated reacted in miraculous fashion; she took up her bed and walked. This is not unusual, but here it was not to prove entirely fortunate: it made us enthusiastic, and enthusiasm, though it is an essential element in ordinary treatment and one to be communicated to the patient, has no place whatever in clinical research. Indeed, the clinical trials of new drugs are so organized as to eliminate this factor altogether by the so-called 'double blind' technique, in which neither the doctor nor the assessor knows whether an active drug or an inert placebo is being used.

For a time we became notorious. For months – this was many years ago – the correspondence columns of the *Lancet* were filled with letters expressing two views: either that G. and I were benefactors of the human race and deserved the Nobel Prize, or, alternatively, that we were bloody liars. The latter view prevailed. An *ex cathedra* anathema was issued by the supreme pontiffs of the rheumatological profession condemning us root and branch and that was the end of the matter. A pity, because buried underneath it all was a fascinating clinical and pharmacological phenomenon which may now never be fully investigated. Its final disappearance was clinched by the timely arrival of cortisone on the clinical scene.

However, G. and I got to know each other thoroughly during the heyday of the investigation. We were swept into a world of high-pressure commercial promotion, gallivanted round Europe at the expense of various drug companies to address scientific meetings, were filmed and fêted. Neither of us ever said or wrote anything we did not believe to be true; but what is truth? In the end I felt thoroughly humiliated; but I survived to realize that humiliation is one of the most valuable experiences a man can undergo. I also recognized how difficult it must be for anyone in the public eye to retain his integrity. On one of our trips, in Paris, the representative of a sponsoring drug company handed us quite a large sum for 'pocket money'. I simply did not know what to do with this and, after some thought, bought a volume of Shelley and handed the rest of the money back.

But I have not yet begun to tell you about G., the wittiest, most sardonic and irreverent of men, the best companion and, incidentally, the best doctor I have ever had the good fortune to meet. Men and women loved him, though he did an immense amount of emotional damage to the latter; and his patients, to whom he habitually referred as 'the enemy' but whom he treated with the greatest courtesy, adored him. When he died, a number of people wrote to me because I had compiled his obituary. The women all declared themselves to have been the love of his life; the men mourned his unflagging gaiety. One recalled their return by troopship from Australia for demobilization at the end of the war: 'We laughed all the way home!' Not a bad epitaph.

G. was a Cambridge man. He had been a mathematician before he took up medicine, and had acquired a passion for statistics which later enabled him utterly to destroy many an unwary writer of medical papers, though he himself wrote little. He had an uncanny diagnostic flair, the gift of recognizing a disease as one recognizes an old friend from a glimpse of his back in the street. But he was not over-enthusiastic about treatment, indeed somewhat nihilistic. He was quite intolerant of fools, and would use four-letter words freely in vituperation to young assistants of either sex who could not, or would not, follow his lucid, patient explanations.

He subscribed to the Cambridge philosophy that 'the best is good enough for me', which is subtly but essentially different from the brasher Oxford attitude: 'Only the best is good enough for me.' His favourite aphorism was: 'Time was made for slaves!', a phrase I ruefully recall each time I fasten the badge of servitude to my wrist in the morning, and he lived his life on that basis, and on the assumption that every desire should be gratified immediately, whatever the expense to himself or anyone else. He travelled hopefully and arrived too often. He was, of course, an alcoholic and therefore the salt of the earth. He was capable of making the most blistering and profane remarks to the eminent of this world to their faces, in public, and deflated many an ego. Like myself, he hated power and those who wielded it with unquenched venom throughout his life.

G. introduced me to an entirely new world: that of the London club. We would sometimes run up to Pall Mall in the lunch hour, feel increasingly guilty as two o'clock approached, knowing that the out-patients were assembling for our afternoon clinics, and then either make an almighty effort to get back, or pass the point of no return and sink into slumber before the fire. There we would wake, first for tea and toast, then for gin and tonic and eventual dinner. (The clinics *were* done, by the registrars.)

G. was not just an alcoholic. He loved wine, about which he knew an immense amount, and made some from his own grapes in Kent. He taught me a great deal about it, beginning with a piece of informa-tion which has always proved of the greatest value; the importance of the imperial pint of champagne. For, as he said – though I think Churchill had said it before him – half a bottle is too little for a man dining on his own and a bottle is too much. Alas, the imperial pint seems to have met its doom with our adhesion to the Common Market, and I have not come across it for many a day. He also explained the biochemical reasons why you become much more stupefied if you drink water in the small hours after a carousal the night before. When we toured together in France, his respect and veneration for the great vineyards was wonderful to behold.

He also loved plants and painting. The immortal W. C. Fields once remarked that there was still hope for a man who hated little children; and, in spite of the havoc that G. wreaked around him in his relations with women, there must be a place in Heaven for a man so devoted to the vegetable world. He was particularly enamoured of camellias and wrote a bibliography about them. And in the series of peregrina-tions which followed the break-up of his marriage, as he moved from one furnished abode to another, he never failed to include in his luggage a dozen of his most prized specimens housed in enormous pots. (I thought this an affectation at the time; but when my own marriage fell to pieces and I had to leave home, I discovered that I could not bear to leave behind some species roses I had introduced, and these too were transplanted on several occasions before being finally abandoned in a rented garden.)

This may be the appropriate place to relate how G. left home. He had the manor house in a small Kent village and enjoyed considerable local fame and respect. On the day of his catastrophic departure he accumulated his luggage, his books and his camellias and sent for the local taxi-driver. Wordlessly they laboured together to transfer these impedimenta into the waiting vehicle. It took a long time, and G. thought he detected behind the driver's impassive features mounting but unspoken accusations of betrayal and dereliction of marital duty. Guilt led him eventually to exclaim: 'I may as well tell you I'm leaving home. The whole village will know about it soon, anyway.' Whereupon the driver burst forth with a heartfelt 'Oh Sir! Oh Sir! I wish I had the courage to do what you're adoing of!' It must also have been about this time, when G. felt his fortunes were at their nadir, that he and I were dining together with a somewhat humourless Scottish pharmacologist at his club. G. remarked that there was one consolation; when you were at the bottom of the pit you couldn't sink any further. Whereupon our literal Scottish friend commented: 'But how d'ye know you're at the bottom, G.?'

The fact was that G.'s attitude to women was hopelessly ambivalent and immature. I shudder to think what an analyst would have made of it. (G. hated analysts and drew attention once in a newspaper to the number of their patients who committed suicide.) It ranged, in temporal succession, from worship and adoration to an almost Apache-like viciousness. He never got it right until he married again towards the end of his life.

We both got stuck on painting at about the same time, the time when our marriages had collapsed. It offered some solace in our distress. I well recall one weekend when I had just remarried and was living in a tiny country cottage. G., who was recovering from a bout of delirium tremens, came for a few days' asylum. One morning we decided to paint a small magnolia tree in the front garden. We established ourselves in the living-room. I began to produce a small, obsessionally meticulous picture. G. set up an enormous canvas and alternately dashed forward to make a brush-stroke and retreated to contemplate its effect. But it was a spring day of alternating sun and shade, and the early magnolia flower opens when the sun shines on it and closes with the clouds. It was not very conducive to reflective painting, and in the end G. rushed out into the garden and shook his fist at the offending tree, shouting: 'I wish you'd make up your bloody mind whether you're going to stay open or shut!'

(Much later, indeed when it was too late to tell him about it, I read about how Monet spent an entire winter painting a gnarled oak-tree until he was overtaken by the spring and the buds burst, upon which the infuriated painter set an army of workmen to removing them.)

G. served in the Royal Navy throughout the war. At one period he was stationed at Scapa Flow and, with time on his hands, invented a disease in which he half believed, and which he entitled 'teetotaller's dyspepsia', on the basis of which he proceeded to invalid an increasing number of ratings from the Service. Their lordships in London got wind of this and despatched an eminent naval psychiatrist, let us say a Rear-Admiral, to investigate the situation. G. received his visitor with equanimity and courtesy. What passed between them was never known, but a few hours later the distinguished visitor was rowed ashore, unconscious and paralytically drunk. The enquiry was never resumed.

G.'s own capacity was incredible. He was fond of relating how, when he arrived in an Australian navy mess during the war, he was met at teatime by a reception committee whose spokesman said: 'Now, you pommie bastard, we're going to start drinking and we'll see who's still on his feet in the morning!' But at breakfast time it was G. who was the sole survivor.

Of course, a rift eventually developed between us, but it was mended, I am glad to think, not long before his death. By this time he had advanced cirrhosis. He had remarried and seemed reasonably content, and the happiest moment of his day, he used to declare, was when he entered his greenhouse in dressing-gown and slippers in the early morning, to greet his plants and take the first gin of the day. He was living on borrowed time and knew it. On the last occasion that I saw him alive at the hospital he referred to his cirrhosis and the hopeless prognosis and said: 'David, if anything happens to me, don't let the bloody surgeons get at me, and don't let them put me in that [expletive] intensive care unit!' As I said earlier, he did not much care for treatment. Immediately after this I had to fly to Nairobi for a few days, and the first remark to greet me from a colleague on my return was to enquire whether I would be going to G.'s cremation. There had been a crisis. He *had* been operated on, twice, and *had* ended his days in the [expletive] intensive care unit. Fortunately he had been unconscious throughout.

I did go to his cremation, on a bitter March day. There had always been a friendly wager between us as to who would live to write the other's obituary, but I was not particularly glad to have won, and anyway I was unable to collect. Both his wives were there. They did not speak; and I could not but recall a bitter little poem by Thomas Hardy about a somewhat similar occasion when the two women wistfully conceded that they might have managed matters better by a less conventional arrangement. Afterwards a few friends drank a lot of whisky in my house and told ribald stories about the departed, which is what he would have wished. But I loved him.

12

'O little child, who cannot choose to live or
die,
I choose for you.

MICHAEL TIPPETT, *King Priam*

'Meanwhile a fire of aloes, cedar and laurel burned between the
legs of the Colossus. Around the circular dais which supported its
feet the children, enveloped in black veils, formed a still circle;
and its arms, abnormally long, lowered its palms to them as if to
seize this wreath and raise it to the skies.

At last the high priest of Moloch passed his left hand under the
children's veils and tore from their foreheads a tuft of hair which
he cast on the flames. Then the men in red cloaks intoned the
sacred hymn:

"Homage to thee, O Sun! Lord of the two zones, Creator self-
created, Father and Mother, Father and Son, God and Goddess,
Goddess and God!"

Before the business began, it was thought fit to try out the arms
of the God. Slender chains reaching from its fingers to its shoulders
continued down behind, where men, pulling on them, made its two
hands rise to elbow level and then come together against its belly;
they moved in stages, in little jerky movements. Then the instruments fell silent. The fire roared. The priests of Moloch moved
about on the great dais, examining the multitude.

An individual sacrifice was needed, a voluntary oblation
designed to influence others. Gradually people approached the
ends of the avenues; they cast into the flames pearls, gold vases,
cups, torches, all their riches; the offerings became increasingly
splendid and profuse. Finally a man, staggering, pale and ghastly
with terror, thrust forward a child; then a small dark mass was to
be seen in the hands of the Colossus; it was plunged into the
gloomy opening. The priests leaned over the edge of the great dais,
and a new chant burst forth celebrating the joys of death and of
rebirth in eternity.

Slowly the children ascended; and the smoke dissipating in great eddies, they seemed from afar to disappear into a cloud. Not one stirred. They were bound at the wrists and ankles and their sombre drapery prevented them from seeing anything and from being recognized.

The brazen arms moved ever more rapidly. They never ceased. Every time a child was laid therein the priests of Moloch spread their hands over it, to charge it with the sins of the populace. As soon as the victims gained the margin of the aperture, they disappeared like a drop of water on a red-hot sheet; and a white smoke rose against the general scarlet.

And still the God's appetite was unappeased. He demanded even more victims. In order to supply him further, they were stacked on his hands and bound round there with a stout chain. Earlier, the devout had wished to count them to ascertain whether their number corresponded to the days of the solar year; but more and more were added, and it was impossible to distinguish them in the vertiginous movement of the horrible arms. This lasted a long time, indefinitely, until the evening. Then the interior walls assumed a darker hue. Then it became possible to discern burning flesh. Some thought they could make out hair, limbs, entire bodies.

The day declined. Clouds massed above the Baal. The fire, now flameless, formed a pyramid of embers reaching up to his knees; red all over, like a giant all covered with blood, he seemed, with his head thrown back, to stagger under the weight of his intoxication.

As the priests quickened their movements, the popular frenzy mounted; the number of victims diminishing, some cried out for them to be spared, others that more were required. The faithful arrived in the avenues dragging their children, who clung to them; and they struck them to make them loosen their grip and to hand them over to the men in red. There were moments when those sounding the instruments had to stop, exhausted; and then the cries of the mothers and the sputtering of the grease as it dripped on the embers could be heard. The fathers of children who had died at some other time cast into the fire their effigies, their toys, their preserved skeletons. Some, who had knives, threw themselves on others. They butchered each other. With fans of bronze the officiants brushed the fallen ashes to the edge of the dais and scattered them in the air, so that the sacrifice might spread over the city, even to the region of the stars.

This great tumult and great light had attracted the Barbarians to the foot of the walls; clutching at which to gain a better view of the debris of the Heliopolis, they watched, open-mouthed with terror.'

Flaubert, *Salammbô.* *

The main difference between ourselves and the Carthaginians is that we destroy the babies before birth instead of afterwards, and burn them dead rather than alive. Also that the guilt, far from being expiated, grows with the crime.

But our Moloch is just as respectable. Men can do anything if a socially acceptable label is applied. The slogan *Arbeit macht frei* over the gate and a brass band to welcome the new arrivals, helped the Germans to close their eyes to what they perfectly well knew was going on in the concentration camps. In the same way, our child murders are done by proper doctors, in proper hospitals. Swift foresaw only too well, in his *Modest Proposal* for using the surplus children of the Irish poor as food, that public shambles would be erected in our cities, and licensed butchers to operate in them would not be lacking.

Why is it socially approved to kill a child before it is born, while it becomes murder to do so a moment after birth? Contrast abortion with the immense care and skill spent in antenatal monitoring of the foetus privileged to survive. Now we can say, for the first time in medical history, that the work of an obstetrician is divided between antenatal and anti-natal care. The medical profession has – largely – supinely accepted a role they formerly rejected with horror, when it would have done them greater honour to have resisted; and this on the ground of bowing to a public opinion which was never more than a publicist's opinion, rail-roaded through by left-wing intellectuals and 'progressive' MPs. And the public little realizes the difficulties faced by courageous and conscientious anti-abortionist doctors and nurses; it may be quite simply impossible for the Catholic gynaecologist who will not undertake to perform 'social' abortions to gain a consultant post.

The 'liberated' woman claims the right to dispose of her own body. She has no such right; there is another person involved; willy-nilly, she is the transmitter of life. I prefer Lysistrata to Moloch; if they do

* My translation

not want children, let them withhold themselves or take the proper precautions. Let me declare my interest. When I was already the father of nine children, my wife became pregnant and we were offered an abortion. It took us much less than twenty-four hours to realize that, if we accepted, we could never live with ourselves or with each other. When her time came, there was an unexpected bonus. After the normal birth of a girl – the only daughter of my own flesh among so many boys – another child was found still in the womb and had to be ripped out by a Caesarean section brilliantly done in the labour-room by a young Yugoslav obstetrician. This little chap was rather knocked about and had to spend a period in an incubator, struggling and panting to survive. Watching him, I understood that, if human beings have any rights – and I am doubtful – the most important is the right to life, and that abortion has struck a massive blow at respect for life. (Was Blake then wrong when he said that all life is holy?)

For me, I have in my old age two delightful and unexpected twins, a gift from the gods, *les péchés de ma vieillesse,* as Rossini said of his later pieces. On abortion, I quote Swift again: 'I never wonder to see Men wicked, but I often wonder to see them not ashamed.'

*

> God gives us leave enough to go when he is
> pleased to reduce us to such a condition that
> to live is far worse than to die.
>
> MONTAIGNE

In the period of classical antiquity suicide was an honourable exit from an intolerable life; it was the Christian Church that was to make it a crime against man and God. There is plenty of evidence. Diogenes called self-murder a reasonable exit, while Seneca said: 'Fortune has no power over him that knows how to die.' (But he allowed death – and this is a point to which I must return – only for those disorders which had long discomposed the functions of the soul.) Horace thought that to compel a man to live against his will, was as cruel as to kill him. (But note that often, for the Romans, the physician was called in to open his client's veins.) According to Montaigne, Pliny recognized three sorts of disease to escape which a man had good title to destroy himself; the worst of which was stone in the bladder with suppression of urine, the great terror of the ancient and mediaeval world. (The others were pain in the stomach and headache, presumably cancer of the bowel and cerebral tumour.) Later we have Lear: 'He hates him / That would upon the rack of this tough world / Stretch him out longer'; and Thomas More, who urged that the tormented sufferer from an incurable disease should either dispatch himself 'or else suffer himself willingly to be rid out of his life by others.'

Suicide is no longer a crime in this country. But encouraging or aiding a person to kill himself may be punishable; and 'mercy killing' remains an act of murder, though judges frequently show compassion when the circumstances are particularly harrowing.

It is essential to understand what euthanasia is and what it is not. As commonly understood, it is a deliberate planned procedure, an act of commission, resulting in death. But it is possible to bring about death in another way, by acts of omission, by neglecting to take those steps which could reasonably be expected to prolong life. One may speak of this as negative euthanasia; it is very different from deciding to do something that is intended to kill.

The kinds of case in which it may be felt that it is better for the individual to die than to go on living fall into well-defined groups:

1. Patients of any age with severe pain – difficult to control by medication or other means – due to progressive, incurable, usually malignant disease.

2. Senile, demented, often agitated and exhausted patients, commonly with incontinence of bowel and bladder and extensive bedsores.

3. Patients of any age with severe brain damage resulting from head-injury or cardiac arrest, whose maintenance in a comatose, vegetable state is entirely dependent on a mechanical respirator.

4. Very severe mental deficiency – usually in children or young adults.

5. New-born children who are 'monsters'; and those with congenital deformities such as very severe spina bifida whose lives can be saved by operation, but who will remain permanently handicapped, in need of repeated surgery, a burden on themselves and their

families.

6. Very old people with severe injuries, usually fractures or burns.

7. Less definable: those with progressive mental or physical disorder leading to eventual helplessness.

In most of these situations death is either imminent or not far off; and in many it is being kept at bay only by unremitting medical and nursing endeavour, by drugs such as antibiotics, and by technical devices such as respirators. Now, in many such cases it is possible to bring about death simply by abandoning these efforts: by not continuing with the drugs or the respirator, by not feeding or caring for the deformed infant, by not resuscitating the elderly cancer patient with cardiac arrest. The patient will die; and this death, though inevitable, will have been brought about at that particular time by an act of neglect for which the attendants are, in theory, legally culpable. Everyone knows that this has always taken place to some extent, quietly and informally, without protocol, at home and in hospital. Nothing is written down, a few words may pass between doctor and nurse, often nothing is said at all. The doctor simply does not prescribe the drug; the elderly brain-damaged patient is not fed through a stomach tube; the hideously deformed child is left untended. The relatives are sometimes, but not always, informed of what is happening.

Then we have a borderline group, also tacitly recognized by doctors and relatives, in which patients suffering from advanced painful malignant disease have their dying accelerated, not by any single act, but by gradually increasing the dose and frequency of pain-killing drugs, usually morphine or heroin, or the celebrated 'Brompton Hospital cocktail' of gin, cocaine, morphine and honey. The patient sinks into a coma and dies painlessly and peacefully.

But nothing so far described is equivalent to positive euthanasia as envisaged by such bodies as the Euthanasia Society, a deliberate single act of homicide to be performed by a physician or physicians at the request of the patient, if he is conscious and of sound mind, or of the relatives, perhaps under the supervision of a medical referee. Its advocates are, essentially, a group of 'enlightened' middle-class individuals who see death as a friendly alternative to prolonged useless suffering. They wish to be able to elect for a painless dispatch at a time of their own choosing if suffering from incurable disease or, alternatively, to express in advance their option for such a solution in the event that they might at some future time become too ill or demented to express an opinion. At the least, they would wish not to be resuscitated in a hopeless medical situation.

Now, so set out, this is, to put it plainly, murder; and it is intended that the act of murder shall be delegated to the medical profession. It is very different from allowing death to ensue by an act of omission; and though it probably takes place already from time to time, it must be far rarer. Admittedly, those who want to legalize positive euthanasia grant the need for stringent precautions and safeguards. There would have to be consent, a valid statutory witnessed request by the sufferer, implying a conviction that he was of sound mind and knew exactly what he was doing. If this were not so, if there were any doubt, consent would have to come from the nearest relatives; and then it would be essential to ensure that their motives were of the purest, unrelated to any pecuniary benefit or to a desire to put an end to an intolerable emotional commitment. We should always have to ask ourselves whether we were taking the decision on behalf of the sufferer or of society.

Now, the euthanasia movement is based on prospective patient demand; it is not primarily medically based, though some doctors support it. But it involves doctors very closely indeed. A doctor's aim is to save or prolong life; euthanasia, like abortion, is the exact opposite of this. One wonders how many doctors would elect, even legally, to kill a patient even when urged to do so by the patient himself. There might be far-reaching effects, eroding the trust of elderly persons in their medical attendants, diluting the efforts one makes in doubtful cases, in those who do not respond to treatment. And, of course, the Catholic view is entirely opposed. One must remember, too, that the option for euthanasia would usually be based on the diagnosis of an inevitably fatal condition. Yet, in one survey, forty per cent of diagnoses were proven incorrect at post-mortem; so that it would be as possible to kill a man in error as to hang him for a crime he did not commit. And medical progress is such that the next few months may bring a cure as yet unenvisaged.

The whole matter of 'consent' is a troubled one. Patients who are depressed and alone frequently ask for death; later, their mental balance re-established, they look back with incredulity to the time when they could ever have made such a request. And then, the middle-aged man who opts confidently for his dispatch when senile, is not at all the same person as the poor confused old dement who may not be able to express clearly his wish to hang on to life. One thinks of those Beerbohm cartoons depicting a dialogue between the youthful and the aged self; the latter, for instance, boasting of the success of his plan in life, and the former replying: 'You mean *my* plan!' In euthanasia we might have the bizarre situation where the aged man is murdered by his younger, more arrogant, self. (Young person: 'Don't worry, I've made all the arrangements for your disposal.' Old person: 'Speak for yourself! I've decided to stick around a little longer.') And, to some extent, euthanasia may simply reflect a present failure adequately to care for the dying. An individual who is miserable, alone, unsolaced and in pain, may not unreasonably elect for death as a socially acceptable form of suicide, but this attitude may change completely under more kindly and efficient management. The desire for death is often passing. Many young persons who suffer paralysis of the lower half of the body from spinal cord injury in traffic accidents often, at the outset, wish to die; adjusted and active again, the will to live reasserts itself.

My own view is that anyone who is able-bodied enough to get around can find means of killing himself; there is always the river, and other ways besides. But the euthanasiast does not want this. He wants civilized, medicated death in bed, the responsibility shrugged off, as ever, on to the unwilling doctor. In a peculiar way, he demands death as *treatment*. And why isn't it considered quite proper to seek death for unending mental anguish, when many of such patients do kill themselves? Is it not because of the recognition that judgment itself is impaired, and is it any less impaired in a state of constant physical pain? The only real indication I might accept for euthanasia is the still lucid and intelligent patient suffering agonizing pain, medically uncontrollable – and this is rare – from incurable disease, and so confined to bed that he is unable to get up and take the final step. And even here, if he can still raise his hand to his mouth, the most the doctor should be empowered to do is wordlessly to leave the tablets by the bedside.

It is a common mistake to imagine that the demented, incontinent old man or woman is miserably unhappy and longing for death. This is not necessarily so. The more ga-ga they are, the less idea they have of what's going on. No, the misery is in the hearts of the beholders, who in their minds compare the patient with what he once was. Also somewhere in their minds is a keen, if unspoken, desire to be finished with the whole sorry business, not to have to pay those painful visits, and also to get the will read. So they may well demand euthanasia on his behalf when it is really on theirs.

To sum up, there is a vast and, in my view, unbridgable distance between not striving officiously to keep alive and taking positive steps to end life. We all acknowledge that the former takes place; the law is willing not to have its attention called to it. We also recognize that death is a part of life, as necessary as sleep; that there is a right time to die, and indeed a general right to die, when well-meant medical interventions are meddlesome and may only make the last few hours or days an unnecessary and useless torment. Sometimes we should just be allowed to die, with as much dignity as we can muster, without having our hearts pummelled or shocked, without needles in our veins or painful or humiliating surgery.

Having said all this, one is only too well aware that there remains a central core of sufferers – alert, intelligent victims of painful incurable disease whose desire to hasten their death is far from unreasonable. But to legislate for these, to ask the doctor to function as a part-time executioner, this bristles with difficulties. And perhaps many doctors would see euthanasia as the beginning of a very slippery slope and recall that Hitler's 'final solution' began with 'mercy killings' of the physically and mentally handicapped in Germany's own institutions and asylums. It is a paradox that 'humane' killing has so far been reserved for animals. Has the time come to apply it to human beings?

I think not. For, as I have said elsewhere, once we are licensed to dispense death and the denial of life with one hand, how efficiently shall we continue to strive in the opposite sense with the other?

13

Sometimes I feel like one of those lop-sided crabs, dwarfed and dominated by a single, enormously hypertrophied claw. Such is the *déformation professionelle* that enables me to function reflexly if set down by a bed with a patient, or to operate effectively however tired or depressed, while remaining unable to cope efficiently with the ordinary affairs of life. I can *respond* to any number of demands; I cannot initiate. My psychiatric friends tell me that, of all groups, it is the doctors who are least able to manage their private lives.* Aldous Huxley once said that continuous proximity is nine-tenths of a successful love affair. True, and it is also nine-tenths of most marital separations. A man must have the knowledge of an alternative, an escape route in life, even if he never uses it. Variety, or alteration, or even just the knowledge that one could make a change if one so desired – these are surely the spice of life. When the salt has lost its savour, it usually means that one has left things too long without renewal. But new need not necessarily mean different; what is familiar can, like the Gospels, be new every day.

Another of life's problems is that what suits us when we start, often differs from what we yearn to do later on, and by then it is usually impossible to do anything about it. We must stay in the same rut until we are thrown on the scrap-heap at sixty-five. The situation is absurd. We ought to be able to have two careers, either in parallel or changing over at forty. In the same way we need two homes and (at least) two wives. Probably I say this because I am not very good at being married, having discovered at thirty that I was illiterate and at forty, when it was too late to change, that I was more interested in words than people. I was delighted recently to come across Robert

* I learn from a senior administrator that 42 per cent of all consultants do not survive until pensionable age, and that 10 per cent have a serious drink or drug problem. 'Nobody who has seen the evidence would underestimate the nature and scale of the problem of the sick doctor.' (*Report of the Committee of Inquiry into the Regulation of the Medical Profession.* H.M.S.O. April 1975).

Louis Stevenson's definition of marriage as 'a sort of friendship recognized by the police', which, he added, 'narrows and damps the spirits of generous men'.

Maupassant is even more poignant on the difficulties and failures of choice in life: *'Que voulez-vous, monsieur, quand on a travaillé toute sa vie, il vient un moment où on s'aperçoit qu'on aurait pu faire autre chose; et alors, on regrette, oh oui, on regrette!'*

Elsewhere he makes an even bitterer comment: *'L'homme actif, vivant et vibrant, se fatigue de tout dès qu'il a saisi la stupide réalité, à moins qu'il ne s'abrutisse au point de ne plus rien comprendre.'* But he was anticipated here by Montaigne: 'Would you have a man sound, would you have him regular in a steady and secure posture? Muffle him up in the shades of stupidity and sloth. We must be made beasts to be made wise.'

This raises the ever-interesting question of whether a medical man may expect to experience difficulties in personal relationships, in his home life, because of the peculiar strains and demands of his work; also whether the capacity to be a really good, even a great doctor, may not rest precisely on his being flawed, the victim of some deformity or deviation of personality.

To take the first point. It is common knowledge that doctors, particularly surgeons, are not always the best husbands and fathers. They are in fact near the top of the league table for suicide, wife-beating, alcoholism and drug addiction. Their work does make physical and emotional demands that tend to leave their wives and children with the dregs at the end of the day. It may well be that the strains of the caring professions, at this time in the twentieth century, are sometimes too great to be borne. As we say, the man who is too good for this world is no good for his wife. He may be adored by his patients and be a petulant tyrant at home; the better he is as a doctor, the worse he may be as a pater-familias.

But it is not just a simple mathematical problem of how much is used up and how much remains, because human beings do not work entirely like that; and many people function *better* at the personal level precisely because they are heavily committed elsewhere. A doctor may complain bitterly of overwork, often with justice, but in many cases he is himself responsible for his work-load. This may be because he sees himself as inexhaustible, omnipotent; because, ageing, he seeks to show himself still active and indispensable; because a reparative urge, the origin of which he does not understand, drives him furiously on. Such a man *attracts* work by osmosis and will be exploited by his less devoted colleagues. I recall struggling to reduce my outpatient appointment waiting-time to zero by doing extra clinics, even at weekends. But all that happened was that work began to flow in from adjacent areas as the news spread to general practitioners that there was a sucker of a consultant who would see patients immediately. It was like my central heating labouring to heat the whole of Sussex because the children leave the doors open. The same with operating. If you regard yourself as irreplaceable, if you can't trust a deputy to do some of the work, if you can't bear to keep a patient waiting because you feel obligated to him, then you will operate all day and every day; the waiting-list is inexhaustible, if you are not, and once again it is the supply that creates the demand. And yet, possibly unfortunately – I am not sure – patients and practitioners will distinguish such a surgeon from those who are merely competent and who do not overtax themselves, and seek to avail themselves of his services.

Further, a man may make use of his clinical responsibilities, onerous as these may be, to justify an inability (but, more often, an unwillingness or an actual fear) to forge and maintain relationships in the home. However burdensome, relations with patients end at the hospital gate; those with wives and children are inescapable. A man may be a saint in the consulting-room precisely because he knows he will see the back of the patient in five minutes, and yet deliberately function as a married bachelor, reserving his limited supply of true warmth for those who will make only transient demands on it. The demands of a wife and family, on the other hand, are limitless. So are a man's inner resources in most cases, if he can see those demands as a means of gaining full human stature instead of as exhausting, menacing, castrating. I did not realize this myself till very late in life. The solution to the kind of middle-life crisis which opened this book is the discovery, at last, that those closest to one are simply human fallible creatures like oneself, to be loved for themselves, not incarnations of earlier figures. The answer to the question so many of us ask in middle life – '*What shall I do to be saved?*' – is, if one is lucky, to be oneself and allow others to be themselves. It is terribly late in life to solve a problem which, for many, never arises; but it is not always too late to mend.

This leads on to the second consideration, to the legend of the wound and the bow; and if you recall that legend you will appreciate that it is possible for someone with an incurable mental or physical affliction, *because* of that affliction, to provide a valuable and indispensable service for others in a way that a more normal individual cannot.

More complex, at a level I am not competent to explore, there are problems of love and hate, envy and guilt, dating from earliest childhood, which may impel a doctor to spend an entire life in an obsessional urge towards reparation. This has been made much of by the psychoanalysts and there may well be some truth in it. I am sure that many persons opt, unconsciously, for a medical career precisely because it affords a socially recognized opportunity to discharge a sense of shame or guilt; that to labour in the slums of great cities or in Asia and Africa may be in the hope of personal salvation. I do think that the devoted man who makes most demands on himself usually does the best work, and that the second-rate have an easier time. But to explain something is not to explain it away, and one may have some understanding of one's motives and still pursue exactly the same course. T. S. Eliot wrote:

> The wounded surgeon plies the steel
> That questions the distempered part
> Beneath the bleeding hands we feel
> The sharp compassion of the healer's art.

But he was thinking of a particular Surgeon.

14

'If a man thinks at all . . . he must be privy
to his own thoughts and desires; – he must
remember his past pursuits and know certainly the true springs and motives which,
in general, have governed the actions of his
life.' 'I defy him, without an assistant,' quoth
Dr. Slop.

LAURENCE STERNE, *Tristram Shandy*

'Tis not all the understanding has to do,
simply to judge us by our outward actions;
it must penetrate the very soul and there discover by what springs the motion is guided.
But that being a high and hazardous undertaking, I could wish that fewer would
attempt it.

MONTAIGNE

It will be apparent to the reader, from hints I have let fall at various
times, that I am no stranger to psychoanalysis. But this does not mean
that I am an advocate of this discipline. Let me explain. I had a 'nervous breakdown' – a severe one – when serving in the Royal Army
Medical Corps during the Second World War. No treatment was
available and I carried on for another year before being invalided. I
do not have to describe the singular and meaningless torments of an
acute anxiety state to those who have experienced them, and I cannot
do so to those who have not. One feels like some creature dredged up
from the sunless depths to face the grey glare of day. Cyril Connolly,
I think, talks of the wires of fear and love being crossed. Perhaps
Coleridge is more penetrating: 'There's no Philosopher but sees /Rage
and Fear are one disease.' Inexplicable recurrent alarm, rising to
panic, the loss of sense of identity causing feelings of depersonaliza-

tion, derealization of the outer world, the inability to invest libido in external objects, obsessional nonsensical and *mad* thoughts and images, insomnia, the lot. The noon-day devil: 'Must I die under it? Is no one near?' The anguish, the isolation, the separation from ordinary human life, from the universe, crushed under the eye of God.

However, I adopted then, and have retained over the thirty odd subsequent years, the attitude that the neurosis is a device to enable one to escape from a frustrating or undesired situation, that it is morally wrong to pay danegeld by escaping from that situation, and that one must soldier on as long as it is evident objectively that one is still capable of reasonable function, whatever the degree of subjective suffering may be. 'For where we are is Hell.' I know. I have been there. I am intimately acquainted with its peculiar delights. Existential dread and depresssion, cosmic boredom, the experience of intellectual disintegration, continuous unrelieved suffering of a peculiarly meaningless and wanton nature – and all these while, to the outside observer, I appeared normally and collectedly engaged in quite strenuous and demanding clinical work. Of course the work – any work – is an enormous help while one is still capable of doing it.

What *is* anxiety? And who am I to attempt to define briefly what authorities have already dealt with at such length? I see it in the light of both the cosmic and the individual situation. The individual is well aware – and simultaneously unaware – of his precarious and fugitive state of existence in the non-human universe, a universe which is indifferent to him (though even to say so much is undesirably anthropomorphic) and to which he is of no account whatsoever. He may paint a face on this universe, usually a religious face, in an attempt to make it more habitable; but the spread of nineteeth and twentieth-century materialism has made this increasingiy impossible for most of us. It is a situation which, seen brutally and objectively, is so appalling that only the bravest can face it without qualms. It is as if, driving unconcernedly along a busy motorway, one suddenly realizes to the full that one is moving at a hundred miles an hour protected only by a thin metal skin from sudden and devastating contacts. And there is really no cure for this. *Y no hay remedia*! It is normally dealt with by adopting the limited blinkered state of consciousness, the parish-pump outlook, which is the precondition of what we call sanity. But when we think of the human condition as it really is, the terror is so great that a more appropriate response under the circumstances would be the flight from reality that is insanity. In Orwellian terms, for human beings Sanity is Insanity and *vice versa*. The only thing that saves us is the mind's inability to embrace that of which it is only a part; we can always fall back on the saving grace of the animal condition. The best we can hope for in general terms is a perplexed obedience to the rules, but rules drawn so loosely as to leave us a disconcerting freedom of action.

In my own case, invaliding from the army became essential and was felt, and is still felt, to have been a degrading defeat incurred in escaping from an undesirable situation. I was recommended by Adrian Stephen – Virginia Woolf's brother – to undergo psychoanalysis; and, living then at Oxford, began a five-day-a-week course of treatment, an hour a day, with a charming and highly intelligent Viennese lay analyst, Eva Rosenfeld, at what must now seem the utterly derisory fee of fifteen shillings a session. (But this was in 1944.) This continued for several years, in the course of which she moved to London once the bombing had ceased and I, perforce, had to follow.

The analysis threw up some very violent images and disturbances. But I rapidly improved in mental health, partly because I was now able to talk things out but mainly, I now see, because I had quitted the stressful situation of military service. Years went by. Mrs Rosenfeld thought we had gone as far as we could together and handed me over to a young medical analyst of Kleinian views. After a time one ceased to think of analysis as anything but a part of the routine of daily life. But the strain, caused in part by the sheer logistics of the situation, was enormous – driving daily right across London after an exhausting day at the hospital, the rapidly mounting expense of the fees, which eventually reached some £600 a year and more. (What must it be now!) And very often I used to fall asleep on the couch in what was the most blissful and expensive slumber and a source of perpetual puzzled enquiry to the analyst of the epoch. I use this phrase because after several further years I was unceremoniously handed over to a Mr X. in Harley Street, like Eva Rosenfeld a lay analyst. By this time, however, I had been divorced and remarried.

The early years with Mrs R. were a happy time, in that tree-shaded study in a nook of St John's Wood. We liked and respected each other, she would sometimes talk of social matters outside the analysis – very reprehensibly no doubt on her part, since the orthodox must not stray from the strict couch situation – and my daily hour was a peaceful haven from the strains of professional and private life and, moreover, a highly intellectualized situation which appealed to me because the intellect is an instrument that one precisely does not use in surgery. (Also, where else can one relax so pleasantly for fifty minutes a day talking about nothing but oneself, that ever-interesting topic, to a sympathetic and intelligent listener, whose bizarre but brief interruptions of one's monologue can readily be ignored?)

The early anxiety state gave way to a chronic neurosis and then, as the years passed, to deepening depression and exhaustion. The attitudes of successive analysts changed – or so it seemed – from a friendly or neutral benevolence to a critical or even caustic view of my alleged incapacity to accept the ordinary facts of existence. The interpretation of dreams and fantasies and behaviour was all very well; but I did not think it was part of an analyst's task to say that I would not or could not face facts, that I had been a silly fool in personal relations, or that, with my enormous burden of clinical work, I was not prepared to shoulder responsibility. It is perfectly true that I am neurotic – which is also part of being a romantic as opposed to a realist. And I intend never to abandon this position, which is best illustrated by reference to a story by E. B. White in the *New Yorker* which, for my money, separates the sheep from the goats. The story is called *The Second Tree from the Corner*. As I recall it now, a middle-aged man is running through his usual list of discontents on his analyst's couch: his dyspepsia, which he fears to be heart-disease, his cancerphobia, problems of work and finance, his deplorable marital situation, his general panic and hopelessness and incapacity. The bored analyst listens dutifully. The question comes up of what one wants out of life and the patient, in an unwonted flash of aggression, demands that the analyst should himself answer that question. Though somewhat taken aback by this reversal of roles, he plays along; he would like a new wing on his house at Westchester, a better education for his children, more holidays abroad. And then, remembering his position, he insists that the patient states what *he* wants. The businessman is at a loss. How can he put into words what it is that tremblingly escapes him in life's dark wood? He looks out of the window; and there is a young tree transfigured by the level evening sunlight, a miracle of translucent and pellucid green, a quivering jewel. Now he knows. 'I want the second tree from the corner, just as it stands!'

Well, I am a 'second tree from the corner' man, and always shall be. I also like cigars and yellow roses, consider the second movement of Mozart's Sinfonia Concertante for violin and viola the most poignant and sublime statement of the human condition (and written at twenty-three!), I infinitely prefer Mahler to Bruckner, like no paintings later than the Impressionists, and think France the best country in the world. Sufficient data to establish my emotional brackets.

Neurosis also has its less acute but still maddening drawbacks. I have never taken a step forwards in life but I wanted to turn back. I suffer badly from Baudelaire's *horreur du domicile*, the perpetual wish to be elsewhere, anywhere but where I am, anywhere out of this world; an increasing desire for absolute solitude, the compulsion to make frequent journeys to remote and inaccessible places. I am not religious and do not believe in an after-life; yet I find it almost impossible to instal myself in this world, which is all we have (as if I really believed in the Celestial City!) Yet there are benefits too: the irresponsibility of distributing one's woes to one's psychiatrist, one's debts to one's accountant and one's worries to one's wife, and then happily going off to do what one really wants to do.

Did my analysis, which continued – with intermissions – for twenty years, do me any good? The difficulty in answering this question is that the patient's definition of cure is not the analyst's. Indeed, the latter regards the very word as rather vulgar. The patient wishes to be well again, to be as he was before he fell, to be more largely and intensely himself, to be able to do capably what he wants when and how he wants. But to the analyst the situation is not at all comparable with that of a patient overtaken by some physical disorder which can be resolved leaving the personality intact. The personality was never intact; it always held its faulty jarring mechanisms, which was why it collapsed in the first instance. Only a radical restructuring will allow anything like normal functioning to continue, for the patient was never well. The first words I recall my analyst saying were the dread sentence: 'Frustration is inevitable!' So what analysis says, in effect, is: 'You must learn to like what you have to do instead of doing what you like, to discard those powerful impulses which you had once regarded as your most personal springs of action.' Anyone who has had anything to do with analysts knows only too well the zombie-like state to which they have reduced themselves; and, self-castrated, they seek to castrate others.* I have not met a single patient who has obtained a cure on his own terms. The best result is a not-too-disgruntled acquiescence with the human condition; all too often there is only what Freud described as the conversion of hysterical misery into ordinary human unhappiness. But I believe in intuition, spontaneity and awareness – that is in joy; and joy is not a commodity to be found on the analytic couch. I can see exactly why a writer like Arthur Koestler could refuse to continue an analysis because it would have deprived him of the drive to unique self-expression.

The patient's personality and thought processes are already disintegrating under the influence of anxiety and very real personal troubles, and the final assault is delivered by the weird and often wounding interpretations of the analyst. At this point of total collapse he is offered as his only hope of salvation the systematized delusions which form the bizarre corpus of analytic theory, and he clutches at these eagerly or reluctantly, if only to appease his tormentor. It is the classical technique of brain-washing, of hysterical conversion.

And, more than that, analysis is, by definition, heartless. There is no sympathy, no support, since the avowed object is to make the patient strong enough and free enough to stand on his own, as if anyone could do so. Therefore the analyst's interpretations are felt as wounding and sadistic criticisms of a human being who is already suffering intensely (as Henry Miller says, no one who has not had a neurosis knows what it is to suffer) and probably with a private life in chaos. The analyst inhibits the taking of any definite steps towards solving these problems, for anything the victim thinks of doing is intrinsically suspect and minutely scrutinized and pulled to pieces.

---

* 'The bourgeois psychiatrist succeeds when his victim is reduced to nothing more than the wretched forsaken condition into which the psychiatrist himself has fallen.' David Cooper, *The Grammar of Living*. Allen Lane, 1974.
  Even more devastating, Thomas Szasz, leading psychoanalyst and Professor of Psychiatry at the State University of New York: 'Psychoanalytic institute: a school where the faculty, composed of old and middle-aged men and women, called psychoanalysts, systematically degrade and infantilize the students, composed of psychiatrists themselves fast approaching middle age, who eagerly submit to this degradation ceremony in the expectation, often unfulfilled, that, after being completely deprived of all independent judgment and the capacity to form such judgment, they will be able to inflict a similar treatment on others, call it psychoanalysis, and charge high fees for it.' *The Second Sin,* Routledge & Kegan Paul, 1974.

And there is an appalling lack of ordinary common sense and humour. I remember, during one of my marriages, an unexpected encounter with a woman acquaintance from abroad under conditions which led us to go to bed on the day we met. When I dutifully reported this at the next session, my analyst expressed total mystification. Had I not already got a perfectly satisfactory wife? I certainly did not and do not regret an episode which did two people a lot of good and no one any harm at all, and detested the solemn naivety of this attitude. When I was divorced, when I forced myself to visit my former home to maintain contact with my sons (separation from whom had been like the wrenching off of my limbs), only too well aware of the nature of the pain that would accompany each parting, I was accused of hanging about my former existence, of not having the courage to look forward.

So cure, in our ordinary terms, there was not and is not. Instead, a sort of stalemate or armistice is reached.

One must always remember that in any treatment, and notably in such a long-drawn-out technique as analysis, at least two essential things happen. Much time passes; and much money passes. The patient makes such a heavy and often crippling financial and emotional investment, over such a long period, that he is compelled to see the process as worthwhile if he is not to admit that the investment has turned out badly. And he is no longer the same person: 'Time is no healer; the patient is no longer here,' as T. S. Eliot says. So it is simply not possible for any patient, or any objective observer, to look or look back at any analysis and say that it was beneficial. The standpoint has shifted.

And yet, what is so strange is that analysis *ought* to be effective. How is it that a process so productive (and it is) of such intellectual awareness, such illuminating flashes of insight, such emotional recall and catharsis, can yet leave the ground–plan unchanged for the better? I think always of the analogy of the tracing of a map which faithfully reproduces the curves and contours of the original terrain but is powerless to redraw them. The rivers will not run back to their source, the path we took that day ineluctably excludes any other choice, the rapids we had to traverse bar our way back. We can see only too clearly where we have been; we still do not know where we are going. As Kierkegaard says, life has to be lived forwards but can only be understood backwards.

And yet, and yet . . . I do not regret my analysis. It helped me to recognize that the world is more than what we see. And when my analyst bluntly called me a silly fool, not a monster, to have made such a mess of my life, perhaps he was right. As Hardy says, if a way to the better there be, it exacts a close look at the worst. But the arrogance of analysts! Their sublime confidence as exponents of a process capable of explaining the totality of human thought and behaviour! And their lack of humour, and often their plain silliness. There is, by the way, an important paradox to be noted here.

Analysis was born in Jewish intellectual circles in Central Europe at the end of the nineteenth century. Some have criticized it on the grounds that Freud's observations of a group of Jewish neurotics in the Vienna of this period cannot possibly be applied to the human race as a whole. I don't take this criticism seriously, for we all go back to Adam, and I notice that such critics are usually perfectly happy with observations made on Trobriand Islanders by Margaret Mead. No, the problem is that analysis, which is the most searching and individual investigation of personal malfunction, should have found its greatest vogue in the USA, where it is as common as it is uncommon in England for a young person to regard years on the couch as a normal part of development. In that country every city has its group of analysts; in England there is (almost) only London. The oddity lies in the fact that in most fields, including medicine, the Americans usually prefer mechanical methods of procedure, reparative mass techniques based on the repair of machines. One would expect American psychiatry to favour drugs, convulsion therapy and cerebral surgery; but, with some fair exceptions, it does not. It is true that there is more money – much more money – in analysis; but perhaps the true explanation is that it is a mass-production technique after all, the belief that analysis provides a ground-plan, a Procrustean blueprint, which can be applied to every individual. With their usual quasi-Teutonic thoroughness, the Americans have, as so often in other fields, developed an imported European idea to its logical, or illogical, extreme.

Finally, to end this discussion, which may have bored some of my readers, analysis does not even begin to satisfy the mandatory requirements for controlled observations used in assessing the results of therapy in ordinary medicine. Results are unquantified, unpublished,

and indeed mostly unpublishable and incapable of statement in protocol form. Freud might have been right when he asserted that
psychoanalysis could 'roll up the neurosis to its source'. Unfortunately, it has long been apparent that he was not. We *know* that
cortisone benefits patients with rheumatoid arthritis because the response is far better than in patients treated with a placebo. And, in my
own case, analysis was a process that had eventually to be abandoned,
while my depression responded immediately to purely physical methods of treatment. And if I feel, to a certain extent, that I am betraying
my past and being uncharitable to my analysts in writing what I have,
it is perhaps because of the enormous and wasted investment I have
already referred to. No one likes to admit to having been a fool, to
have served his seven years for Rachel and found only Leah in the
wedding-tent. I know – and I think most of us know nowadays – that
psychoanalysis is a useless, exhausting, often dangerous, and *obsolete*
waste of time, energy, money and spirit.

*

I know 'tis but a dream, but feel more anguish
Than if 'twere truth. It has been often so.
Must I die under it? Is no-one near?
Will no-one hear these stifled groans and wake
me?

COLERIDGE, *The Nightmare Death in Life*

'Tis a disease particular to man . . . to hate
and despise himself.

MONTAIGNE

To wake at three in the morning, without hope of subsequent
sleep. To be preoccupied with mournful obsessions, the sad teasing
of fragments of flesh on the old bones; or frank despair; or else – so
close are heaven and hell – the mind racing with lucid intelligence, a
benevolent hypomania, a state in which the writer must get out of
bed and write, capitalizing on his depression, now that it has swung

to the other axis, turning his illness to good purpose. Or one can do a lot of gardening, in summer, between five o'clock and breakfast.

Many a depressive has suffered years of insomnia, followed by day-time fatigue and collapse, until cured by an intuitive doctor and a handful of pills; or else the depressive equivalent, the hypochondria which masks the essential illness with obsessive complaints of somatic pains, of visceral dysfunction.

The will cannot overcome these tortures, though it serves to endure them, for it is the will itself that is diseased. A disturbance of a peripheral sense-organ, the eye or ear, alters our perception of the physical world but leaves our mental life undisturbed. But when the biochemistry of the brain undergoes its periodic change, our very experience of the universe alters; the target organ that malfunctions is what we live by. In depression one sees through a darkened window; but one *is* the window. Life loses its meaning, the will to endure wavers, nothing is worthwhile. Instead of rising to greet the day with anticipation, we are at best, like Boswell: heavy, confused and splenetic, queasy and despondent, aware that this can be dispersed by vigorous physical or intellectual exercise, and yet 'when one is in low spirits he generally is so indolent and careless that he will just sink under the load.'

Often we find the prospect terrifying; the figures on the station platform brood with menace, we cannot communicate. No one can understand this who has not experienced it; and what is worse, we ourselves, in our healthier periods, can only recall this state as obscurely as we remember pain. Whatever else it may be, the brain is the organ of suffering; and when this function is in abeyance, there is nothing corresponding to the mind's eye to summon up our past experience because there is nothing proximal to the brain that has suffered.

The problem, the dichotomy in treating depression lies between quite opposite poles: Can a few pills satisfy the soul's need? Can mere words deal with a disordered cerebral biochemistry? But it is not as clear-cut as this; both factors operate. The psychoanalysts – even such a humane one as the late Donald Winnicott – have gone on record as saying that we have the right to suffer, and that this right should not be taken away. How can they maintain this, now that we can to a considerable extent abolish this misery with drugs or electrical convulsive therapy? Is it immoral to remedy a biochemical disturbance by biochemical means? Admittedly, ECT is as crude and empirical as kicking a malfunctioning television set; and, admittedly, any physical treatment of a disordered mind may be felt as degrading. Yet, if we are only dealing with a sperior kind of machine, then mechanics are necessary. The implicit objection is that, if depression and despair are due to physical factors, this may apply also to our higher and happier mental states. I do not see why we need fear this, now that this century has shown so clearly how readily freedom and dignity may be destroyed by the physiological perversions of torturers. Let us rather enjoy the good times, whatever their origin, the intrinsic excellence of a machine that runs sweetly and smoothly. Anyone who has just got over a migraine attack will know what I mean.

(It is interesting that one group of anti-depressant drugs – the mono-amine oxidase inhibitors – work by suppressing the action of the enzymes that oxidize away certain biological amines. Why this should be so is not clear. But under such a regime the amines accumulate, and if there is added a rich supply of food amines from cheese or broad beans or pickled herring, there is an acute episode of rising arterial blood-pressure which, at best, resembles an attack of migraine to the n-th degree and, at worse, may provoke fatal cerebral haemorrhage. I have had such attacks when alone in the wilds of Yugoslavia, on a Danish beach – when I was so full of anticoagulants after a recent coronary episode that I knew, if a blood-vessel gave way, I should bleed to death – and by my own fireside. I say it is like migraine, but as like as a thunderstorm resembles the rattling of a tin sheet; one wonders, however, whether migraine sufferers are deficient in essential enzymes, and if their attacks can be triggered off by such foods. And they are and they can be. So perhaps our experience with anti-depressants is beginning to open a door through which can be glimpsed a hope of controlling migraine attacks and preventing their recurrence.)

I in no way wish to decry the importance of psychotherapy in depression; it can be very valuable. But below a certain depth of ill-ness useful communication is simply impossible; and one of the virtues of drug treatment is precisely that it can lift the patient back to a level at which words may be useful.

There is also an existential view of depression. Anyone who has lived in a village will have known taciturn, reserved individuals who plod through life with difficulty in some simple role. They often lodge with married couples, few of them hang themselves in the woodshed, they have the silent, often affectionate support of the community. But translate these same villagers to urban conditions and such men would at once become cases of severe clinical depression; and many of the previously 'normal' villagers would themselves exhibit overt features of this illness under the enhanced pressures. This is where both the drug doctors and the psychotherapists perhaps err in common; they tinker with the individual and his brain and assume the society that generates such strains to be immutable, when, possibly, it is the society itself which is in need of treatment. I know that, on those (rare) occasions when I have got my conditions of living the way I want them, my psyche has given me little or no trouble.

Finally, one may wonder whether depression is compatible with responsible work in many fields. The fact is that it is those who are most conscientious and perfectionist about their work who tend to suffer from this disease, and yet are capable of carrying on to a remarkable extent under the double burden. Montaigne quotes Plato's dictum that melancholic persons are the most capable of discipline and the most excellent. Of course, short of suicidal despair, even depressives have their moments. Cheerfulness breaks in. As Hardy wrote: 'The tendency to be cheered is stronger than the tendency to be cast down; and a soul's specific gravity constantly reasserts itself as less than that of the sea of troubles into which it is thrown.'

And, of course, depression is closely linked with creativity. As Roethke says: 'In a dark time the eye begins to see.' Or Jeffers: 'Better invent than suffer.'

15

Soles occidere et redire possunt; nobis cum semel occidit brevis lux, nox est perpetua una dormienda.*

CATULLUS

My theory is to enjoy life, but my practice is against it.

CHARLES LAMB

I want to write about my philosophy of life; and yet, for much of my life, the question would have had no meaning. Like most of us I lived reflexly – which is the precise opposite of reflectively – and would have found it odd, and still do to some extent, to be told that there are individuals who plan their lives and behaviour to a deliberate scheme of things.

Yet, in another sense, every man must have a philosophy, even if it is no more than the formulation of his personality. He must be presumed to intend the probable consequences of his actions, and he acts in a certain way. To apply this to myself, or at any rate to my work, I can do no better than have recourse to certain authors who seem exactly to exemplify the way I have lived.

One is George Eliot. F. W. H. Myers tells us that, replying to questions about the great issues of life and death, 'She, stirred beyond her wont, and taking as her text the three words which have been used so often as the inspiring trumpet-calls of men – the words *God, Immortality, Duty* – pronounced, with terrible earnestness, how inconceivable was the *first,* how unbelievable the *second,* and yet how peremptory and absolute the *third.'*

I have suffered a good deal from neurosis and depression and the pain of loss. Who hasn't? But I agree more and more with Unamuno

* Suns may set and rise again; but to our brief light, when once it sets, comes a night that must be passed in never-ending sleep.

195

when he says that suffering is the substance of life, the badge of all our human tribe, and that it is only suffering that makes us persons. 'And suffering is universal, that which unites all of us living beings . . . the religious anguish that flings us upon the bosom of God, there to be watered by the divine tears.'† One does not have to be a theist to accept the validity of this statement; perhaps Dostoyevsky was right when he said that Man may need suffering as much as he needs happiness. I now see that I have never accomplished anything worthwhile, in surgery or literature, except in the depths of despair, and that the periods of contentment were relatively fallow. Creativity and happiness are no bed-fellows. In my work, suffering has proved an unfailing spur and the work itself has been a consolation. It has also been of the greatest value in the clinical situation because of my insight into the travail of others, and because no patient has ever been able to say to me: 'You don't know what it is to suffer !' Most of them recognize this intuitively, and it is very important for the therapist and the patient to share this experience.

So that, in my case, as in that of many another surgeon, to quote George Eliot again: 'No wonder the sick-room and the lazaretto have so often been a refuge from the tossings of intellectual doubt – a place of refuge for the worn and wounded spirit. Here is a duty about which all creeds and all philosophies are at one; here, at least, the conscience will not be dogged by doubt, the benign impulse will not be checked by adverse theory. Here you may begin to act without settling the preliminary question . . . where a human being lies prostrate the moral relation of man to man is reduced to its utmost clearness and simplicity.'

Unamuno puts it another way: 'All of us, each one of us, can and ought to determine to give as much of himself as he possibly can – nay, to give more than he can, to exceed himself, to go beyond himself, to make himself irreplaceable, to give himself to others in order that he may receive himself back again from them. And each in his own calling or office. The word office, *officium,* means obligation, debt; and that is what we always ought to mean in practice.'

Now, looking back, I see that I have lived my professional life on this basis. It is the life of obligation, so destructive – as I have learned

† Miguel de Unamuno. *The Tragic Sense of Life,* transl. J. E. C. Flitch. Macmillan, London and Basingstoke, 1954.

to my cost – of the emotions. But where did this drive come from?

I think of my father, of his immense industry, his stern sense of family duty, his unfailing kindness to others, often to his own despite; and I know that these qualities, imprinted in childhood, served to sustain me through the strains of surgical life. I have never turned away a patient because I was too tired or too busy; I have always done more than was expected of me or was reasonable, because that is how I visualized my father: unflagging, heroic, unsparing in energy, yet also coarse and despicable at times, as I am myself. I am ashamed to recall that in analysis, and expected to bear witness to the conflicts of the oedipal situation, I supplied the required material with gusto. There *were* conflicts; I was never close to him. But when he was dying I realized how much I had loved him. It was his example that led to the childhood conviction that there was no limit to what an adult human could do; so that, on days when I have risked destroying my-self by operating for ten or twelve hours at a stretch or seeing innumerable outpatients, it has been in the sure belief that *he* would have been equal to it. It may be true that there was also envy and rivalry, the desire to surpass; but any other model would have been easier to choose, and it is by emulation that we learn and grow.

In a wider sense, I suppose that my philopsophy is existentialist. I see no order or meaning in life, no moral order in the universe other than that which we ourselves choose to put there. Like George Eliot I find God and immortality inconceivable and unbelievable, a charm-ing but pathetic illusion of the childhood of our race. Yet it is con-venient at times to behave as if God existed, and most atheists are really in a rage with him for *not* existing.

I have already – now that for me the world has become a picture-gallery in which the portraits are being changed too often – spoken of my constant preoccupation with the fear of death, which seems to me to be terribly unfair. Unamuno quotes Sénancour: 'Man is perish-able. That may be so; but let us perish resisting . . . if it is annihilation that awaits us, let us not so act that it will be a just fate.' Unamuno suggests changing this to the active form: 'Let us so act that it will be an unjust fate . . . so as to make our annihilation an injustice, to make our brothers, our sons feel that we ought not to have died; that is something within the reach of us all.'

That leads on to questions of freedom in human life. What is im-portant is not whether we really are free, but whether we *feel* free.

The fact is that we are all trapped in our flesh, our mortality, within the physical laws of the environment, in marriages, professions and parenthood. But within this framework there is a great freedom of manoeuvre. We have to accept the rules of chess – the shape of the board, the permitted movements of the pieces – but, having done so, the range of possibilities is infinite, or infinite enough for human beings. No one chess-game is like another. So we come to Hegel's iron paradox: 'Freedom is the knowledge of necessity.' We have to begin by acknowledging the rules of the game – which remain the rules even if we deny or defy them – and then play the game for its own sake. A man is free in an existential sense, the end-product – so far – of a non-human universe, lacking a creator, puny and short-lived, but able within these limits to order his own destiny, to introduce a personal concept of meaning into chaos, and even perhaps, ultimately, to become God, to acquire the immortality, omnipotence and omni-science he originally attributed to deity because they were what he most wanted; and this by his own efforts. The universe can mean, in Humpty Dumpty's terms, anything we choose it to mean.

But I wish I could reconcile this intellectual awareness of our essential loneliness with my very occasional acceptance of moral order and benevolence in the universe, the times when we think: 'Ah, how this world suits me!', when we ought rather to have thought that the reverse is true, that it is we who suit the world, which has conditioned our evolution. We say 'Thank God' automatically and experience Freud's 'oceanic' feeling that all's well and for the best in a personal universe, as if human self-sufficiency were merely a convention we use to live by and the real truth lay elsewhere.

I am preoccupied with the transience of human life, and those authors and composers who most appeal to me are those who best convey this poignancy: Housman, Hardy, Delius. All very adolescent, no doubt, but who is to say that adolescence – when we exchange eternity for identity – is not the most important stage of life. I find it difficult to listen to Mahler's *Das Lied von der Erde* without tears, and recall – or seem to recall – Kathleen Ferrier singing this when she had already had an operation for an illness which she must have guessed would prove fatal, so that the pathos of the recurrent *ewig . . . ewig* in the last movement of farewell was almost unbearable.

The illogicality of a complaining attitude to life and death lies in its assumption that there is someone to complain to; and there isn't.

But I admit to resentment at times. What are we?

Man is a highly percipient mammal, the only one who walks upright, looks at the sky, contemplates the past and anticipates the future at the expense of the present moment, works, suffers, laughs and cries, knows he is going to die, kills his fellows and buries his dead. But also, Housman says:

> From far, from eve and morning,
> From yon twelve-winded sky
> The stuff of life blew hither
> To knit me, here am I.

On this view a human being, like all living things, is no more than a fortuitous concatenation of atoms, met together by chance and soon to be dispersed. That these atoms of the flesh are themselves immortal is no consolation, for it is unlikely that a precisely similar grouping will ever recur to house the same spirit. If this were all, if, like Hardy's thrushes, we were so short a time ago just water, earth and air and will soon be so again, then life is indeed like the bird flying briefly through the lighted Saxon hall. But there is more to it than that. For one thing, the unique combination *did* turn up. Each of us *is* that far-off divine event to which the whole Creation moves. And then, the atoms themselves are not so important as the fact that they are, most improbably, *organized* by life into a protoplasmic whirlpool which remains recognizably the same though its constituent particles are being continuously replaced. Personality depends on, or is the expression of, a physical substructure; but this is always in flux. Yet the organization that controls all this is handed down in coded form from one generation to another; is this not immortality? So that each of us has a lineage going back to the beginnings of this planet, if not before; and it does seem a bit hard that we should be extinguished just as we are learning how to behave. My bitterest regrets relate to my unkindness to those I love. I think of that terrible remark of Frederick the Great: 'Miserable madmen that we are, with only a moment to live we make that moment as harsh as we can.'

Life is a journey during which we may not halt. I have never encountered a better description of this journey than the following passage by Walter de la Mare:

A man picks up his candle, and in its clear but baffling light must push his way through the darkness of life's corridor past every hindrance, stopping his ears as best he can against fear and the conflicting voices, towards the glimmer of the window at the far end, only to stand at last confronting in the dark glass, against the deeper darkness of the night without, his own weary and haunted face, bravely aware that even the candle that has been his guide and comrade must be extinguished before he can see beyond.

There is a place for despair in life, if it is the creative despair that masters impossibility, begets the hope that 'through its own wreck creates the thing it contemplates'. Time and Death conquer all and are very strong; but Love and Thought are nearly as strong. For the time being, I go on. And at the end? Must it be? It must be.